Tarot for Fiction Writers

A Writersaurus Guide
By Haley Dziuk

Copyright information

ISBN-13: 978-1-947094-13-0

www.thewritersaurus.com

Table of contents

Introduction

Have you ever had a really great story idea, but were unable to flesh it out into a full-fledged narrative? If you're a pantser (someone who writes by the seat of their pants), you may have written a dozen pages before getting stuck. If you're a plotter (someone who plots their novel out before writing), you probably haven't started writing yet, because you know in your gut an essential piece of the story is missing, the plot element that will take it from "ok" to "amazing."

Then one day the answer hits you. The amazing plot twist that readers will never see coming but makes total sense, the character flaw that will make your protagonist oh-so-relatable, or the complication that keeps your heroine from sharing her feelings with her love interest. *Aha! Why didn't I see that sooner?* You think as you sprint for your computer or note pad.

Every writer has these moments and the elation that accompanies them. It's like having a muse whisper directly in your ear. For most, these eureka moments happen only rarely, with no pattern as to what sets them off. You might not even be actively working on writing. You could be walking your dog or taking a shower. (Personally, I've had a freakish amount of them while standing in line at amusement parks.)

What if I told you there's a way to *trigger* these moments to happen? That you no longer have to wait for the whims of the muses to turn in your favor?

That's what the tarot can do for you.

If someone told me this a year ago, I would have laughed. My grandmother gave me a couple tarot decks when I was young, but apart from a few Halloween parties, they spent the majority of their time in my possession languishing in a closet. Though I was skeptical of their purported uses, I was still drawn to them and could never bring myself to throw them out.

Fast forward to last summer. I was up against a tight deadline, but was stuck on a plot point in my story. No matter what I did, I couldn't seem to connect the pieces of my story to make it go where it needed to. It was during a procrastination session on Pinterest that I came across a storyteller's spread.

The idea that you could use tarot as a writing tool seemed like a novelty at best, but what did I have to lose? I pulled out one of my decks and laid out a few cards.

At first, the cards didn't seem to be connected in any way, either to each other or to the story problem I was facing. Still, I stared at the cards, thinking.

And then it hit me: the answer to the story. It was perfect, and once I saw it, totally obvious, too. It felt like I'd been blocked because my subconscious was waiting for me to catch up and see it.

I immediately jumped on my computer and started writing, and I didn't stop until the story was done. At first, I thought this must be a fluke, but in the few months between that first spread and now, I've had dozens of such moments.

Even the spreads that don't reveal a major development such as the one I just described help me learn about my plot, characters, and world. I haven't done a single spread that felt wasted. More than that, laying out a tarot spread puts me into an energized, creative "flow" state. I'm better able to focus on my story and the writing process, whereas otherwise I often feel distracted.

So I've become something of a convert. I still consider myself an analytical person, but I can't deny the benefits the tarot has brought into my writing life. I hope to bring these benefits to you, too.

Are you ready to unlock your creativity to discover engaging, realistic characters and jaw-dropping storylines? Then read on!

Why the Tarot?

You may be wondering if you have to believe in the tarot as some all-seeing oracle that's capable of predicting the future to reap its benefits as a writing tool.

The short answer is no, you do not.

Most psychics would tell you that the tarot is used to focus your own mental power, rather than being innately powerful itself. When we use them as a writing tool, we're focusing our *creative* energy.

The truth is, the tarot is specifically equipped to help us develop stories. There are character cards, situation cards, and archetype cards, many of which bear striking resemblance to parts of the hero's journey and other plot structures. This makes sense—stories mirror life, after all.

What's in This Book

This book is divided into three parts. Part I is a quick guide to getting started, including choosing a deck and tarot journal. Even if you already have both of these things, I suggest skimming through this section.

Part II is all about the cards. Even if you're familiar with the tarot, there's information there that's specific to using it for story creation. To make this book more accessible, I have created an appendix with suggested meanings for each card. One deviation from most tarot books is that I break the Minor Arcana into two sections—"character" cards and "situation" cards.

In Part III, I go into the nitty gritty of conducting readings and how best to use the tarot in your writing. This includes several "spreads"—a spread is the shape you lay out cards in to do a reading. For each spread, I give a brief explanation for the narrative theory behind it, then detail the spread itself. Part III ends with a section on creating your own tailor-made spreads.

At the end of the book you will find a list of resources, a glossary, a list of the card meanings, and links to all the free downloads mentioned throughout the text. Since I know you may not have time to do the exercises and spreads as you read, I've collected each in an own easy-to-access appendix at the end. That way you don't have to search through the book to find them. (You will do the exercises, though, won't you?)

About the Writersaurus

Before we get started, I want to tell you a little about The Writersaurus and myself, so you have some idea about the person who's telling you all this stuff.

Thewritersaurus.com is a website dedicated to educating writers and creatives of all types about all aspects of writing, editing, publishing, and marketing. When I started the site four years ago, I had no idea what form it would take—I only knew it would center around writing.

The site quickly found its shape as the place where I shared everything I learned about writing, editing, and publishing in real-time. It kept me accountable, and more importantly, forced me truly internalize the information. Without it, I would not be the writer that I am today. Thank you for being a part of that journey!

About Me

I am a writer just like you. I've been writing books, essays, and stories since I was in grade school, but it wasn't until April 2017 that I started to take writing seriously as a possible career path. That's when I decided to finally write and publish the weird west serial that had been kicking around my brain for nearly half a decade. Three months later, the first episode of *Jeremiah Jones Cowboy Sorcerer* hit the virtual shelves.

Currently, I write in the fantasy and horror genres—and now nonfiction, too, I guess. At the time of this book's writing, I've written and published ten books, and have several more that I will start after this book is done, all of them developed with the techniques described in this book. You can learn more about my fiction at hdukeauthor.com.

Part I: Getting Started

Choosing Your Tarot Deck

First things first: This book won't do you much good without your own set of tarot cards. If you do not already have a deck, there are several routes available to you. The first is to head to the store. The more popular decks, such as the Rider-Waite deck, are available at any Barnes and Noble. Smaller New Age stores will have a more curated selection. You will find the widest range of choices online; there are hundreds of tarot decks out there. At least a few are bound to fit your tastes and budget.

If you need to wait for shipping, or frankly, aren't sold on the whole tarot thing yet, you have a few other options. One is to use a normal deck of playing cards. You *can* do readings with them, but there are areas where the fifty-two-card deck falls short. For example, the lack of illustrations makes remembering the cards' meanings much less intuitive. I give a basic introduction to reading with playing cards after the list of card meanings on page 98.

Another option is a printable deck. There are both free and paid versions out there. I'd recommend the Court Tarot, which is beautiful and available to download for free from the Dark Tarot website at darktarot.com/printable_tarot_deck.

The last route is an online tarot spread generator. There are a few out there if you do a web search. I haven't used any, so I can't recommend them—or promise that they won't infect your computer with adware. A safer bet may be a tarot app. Just be sure to check the app's description and rating before you hit download to make certain it fits your needs.

Virtual decks are okay for getting your feet wet, but they shouldn't be relied upon long-term. Our main purpose in this book is to unlock your creativity. Feeling the cards under your fingers as you shuffle is part of that.

I found my first tarot deck at my grandmother's house when I was eleven. It was the 1971 reprint of the Rider-Waite deck, still the most popular deck of all time. Even those who know nothing about the tarot will recognize much of its imagery.

The Rider-Waite deck follows the most common tarot format, meaning it has seventy-eight cards total—twenty-two in the Major Arcana and fifty-six in the Minor Arcana. If that sounds like gibberish, don't worry. I'll elaborate on the Major and Minor Arcana in Part II. For right now, you just need to know that the seventy-eight-card or "standard" deck is the most common version, and also the one I recommend for use with this book. While the illustrations for each deck vary, the cards will have the same names (The Fool, The Magician, Death, etc.).

Some decks deviate from the seventy-eight-card format. These are usually called "oracle" decks, though you'll also see them referred to as "non-standard" or "non-traditional." You can certainly use those cards for the spreads in this book, but you'll have to refer to the booklet that comes with them for their meanings. Make sure you read the product description thoroughly before you buy so you know what you're getting. Most will tell you how many cards there are. If the number is anything other than seventy-eight, you're not getting a standard deck.

The Rider-Waite deck is by far the most popular and easy to find. However, there are plenty of other lovely decks out there. Many decks are self-published, if that's something you're interested in. Most follow the same standard format as the Rider-Waite deck, and they have similar images and meanings. There are decks inspired by the works of Shakespeare, *The Wizard of Oz,* and *The Lord of the Rings,* among others. There's even a tarot deck with illustrations that all feature gummy bears! The most important thing is that the imagery in the deck speaks to you personally, and is conducive to the genre(s) and tone(s) you write in.

I now own several decks, including the one I found at my grandmother's house so long ago. (It's now missing a few cards after an encounter with an overenthusiastic Labrador Retriever.) The deck I use most often is the Robin Wood Tarot. It follows the seventy-eight-card format, and the images manage to be original while still retaining the spirit of the Rider-Waite deck.

So now you have a bit of background information that will help you choose a tarot deck. Are you ready for your first exercise?

Exercise 1: Choose a tarot deck. Search online or visit your local book shop or New Age store. Spend some time looking at sample art. Do you like the images and symbols, and do they spark your creativity?

Once you've bought them, flip through the cards and familiarize yourself with the imagery. Don't worry about the meanings yet.

Your Tarot Journal

The second thing you'll need is a tarot journal—any notebook will do. Make sure it's comfortable to write in.

Like most writers, I own more journals than I could ever hope to fill. The majority were gifts and are quite lovely. Still, I always seem to end up writing on some ratty memo pad or the blank pages in the back of my high school geometry notebook—the cheap kind where the wire gets untwisted and becomes a safety hazard. It's like I have a mental block or something.

It's better to keep a journal dedicated only to the tarot. That way, when you need to reference a spread, they'll all be in one easy-to-find place, and you won't have to flip through five notepads to find what you're looking for—not that I know from personal experience, or anything. I don't recommend keeping your tarot journal digitally. It's easier to remember information after you've written it down by hand. If you want a digital record of your spreads, write them by hand first, then type them out later.

After I finished the first few revisions of this book, I realized that many people might want a guided version, so I created *The Fiction Writer's Tarot Journal,* which contains prompts, exercises, and worksheets for each section of this book. It's now available on Amazon. You can also download a free printable version by visiting insert www.thewritersaurus.com/freetarotjournal.

Exercise 2: Choose your first tarot journal and label it as such. Don't forget a writing utensil!

Part II: The Cards

On Learning the Card Meanings, and a Brief Note on the Order of This Book

In the first drafts of this book, this section included a list of individual card meanings. After some feedback from a beta reader, I realized that this implies that you have to memorize all the meanings before you could start using them.

Let me state this clearly: **You do not have to memorize each card before you start!** Obviously, once you do have the cards memorized, readings will be easier and more automatic. That will come in time. The best way to really learn your cards is to use them. To make this easier, I've included a "cheat sheet" list of all the card meanings in the back of the book. I have also created a PDF version that you can print out and have nearby. Visit www.thewritersaurus.com/tarotdownloads to download it.

There are certain things about the deck that you *do* need to know for the section on readings to make sense. That information is below. We'll start with an overview of the two major components of the standard deck, the Major and Minor Arcana.

The Major Arcana

When most people think of the tarot, the images and symbols that come to mind are from the Major Arcana. They are the sexy cards, the ones with the flashy pictures and grandiose symbolism. Some of the most famous Major Arcana cards include Death, The Devil, The Fool, and The Magician. There are twenty-two Major Arcana cards in total.

Unlike the Minor Arcana, which represent either characters or smaller, everyday moments, each Major Arcana card either represents a character archetype or a major, paradigm-shifting event.

The Minor Arcana

The cards of the Minor Arcana represent everyday situations and people. The Minor Arcana is divided into four "suits"—Cups, Wands, Swords, and Pentacles.

Each suit is associated with a certain element:

Cups = water

Wands = fire
Swords = air
Pentacles = earth
The suits each have their own themes, as well:
Cups = emotion and relationships
Wands = action and creativity
Swords = intellect and logic
Pentacles = material wealth and practical matters
In fiction, groups of people are often divided into four categories. One example is the houses in *Harry Potter:*
Cups = Slytherin
Wands = Gryffindor
Swords = Ravenclaw
Pentacles = Hufflepuff
Or the factions in *Divergent:*
Cups = Amity
Wands = Dauntless
Swords = Erudite
Pentacles = Abnegation
Each suit contains fourteen cards, ten cards numbered one through ten, and four "court" cards (King, Queen, Knight, and Page).
If you think the Minor Arcana sounds an awful lot like a regular deck of playing cards, you'd be right. In fact, playing cards and tarot cards have very similar histories. The four suits of the tarot correspond directly to the suits of the playing card deck:
Cups = Hearts
Wands = Clubs
Swords = Spades
Pentacles = Diamonds
This is fairly easy to remember. Hearts deal with emotion, as do the Cups; both "wand" and "club" are fancy names for a stick you hit someone with; swords and spades are both pointy weapons; and pentacles, otherwise known as coins, are a form of wealth, just like diamonds.
If you don't mind missing out on the Major Arcana, you can use a regular playing deck for the spreads detailed later in the book. I talk about this process on page 146.

Important Terms: "Upright" and "Reversed"

Two terms you need to be familiar with are "reversed" and "upright." These both refer to the way a card is facing when it is laid out. Upright means that a card is right-side up; reversed means it's upside down, as shown in this diagram:

upright   reversed

This concept is important because a card's meaning changes if it is reversed. Generally, when a card is reversed, it is interpreted as having either an opposite or extreme version of its upright meaning.

Reversals are very pertinent when using the cards for writing. Stories so often deal with opposites and foils. In more complex stories, a character's fatal flaw is often an otherwise positive quality taken to an extreme.

Consider both a card's upright and reversed meaning whether it was upside down or not because ALL situations have positive and negative aspects, just as character's traits can be both positive and negative.

For example, a character might be described as having a good work ethic. This work ethic may drive him to great success in his professional life. The reversal of this is that his personal life and health may suffer. His friends and family may even call him a "workaholic."

Of course, it's up to you whether you want to consider both sides or not, or even use reversed meanings at all.

Exercise 3: Separate out the Major Arcana from your deck. Using the descriptions above (or the ones listed in the booklet that came with your deck), go through the cards one by one and try to relate their descriptions or imagery to your story in some way. If you are not currently working on a story, try to relate them to books, television shows, or movies. The purpose of this is to start seeing the cards through a narrative lens.

Exercise 4: This is the most beneficial exercise in this book! During the course of your tarot journey you'll want to write down the meaning of each card in your tarot journal **by hand**. I suggest starting by going through the cards in your deck one by one, and pulling out two or three cards that appeal to you. Before looking up their meanings, consider each card and write down your impressions of it (writing out a description of the card's illustration REALLY helps you remember its meaning!). Then refer to either the card meanings section on page 98 or the pamphlet that came with your deck.

Repeat this process over the course of a few weeks until you've written meanings for each card.

Be sure to order the entries in such a way that you can easily find them later.

Tarot Tip:

As you get acquainted with and use the cards, your understanding of their meanings will deepen. Continue to write these insights down in your journal.

Part III: Conducting Readings

Now we get into the thing you've all been waiting for—using the cards! The first subsection gives an overview of reading the cards, including a few dos and don'ts. After that, we go into the spreads themselves.

A Brief Note on Realistic Expectations

As stated earlier, the benefit of using the tarot as a story generation tool is that you can trigger story ideas rather than wait for them to spontaneously occur. You can do in a day or two what usually takes much longer. When you're regularly using the tarot for this purpose, your subconscious will actually start to associate the cards with that creative state, and you'll be able to enter it more easily.

That said, it's not a magic bullet. Don't expect to lay out the cards once and suddenly have a story. This takes time and creative thought, especially when you're first starting out. If you try to sit down and force out a story while staring at the cards, you'll stifle the creativity you're trying to foster. Instead of provoking a heightened creative state, you'll start to associate the cards with frustration and blockage.

So relax and try not to be too serious.

When to Use the Tarot

There are several ways writers can use the tarot for story creation. I most often use it while prewriting. For clarity's sake, I'll refer to this phase as "brainstorming" throughout the book. While brainstorming, the story is nowhere near complete. If you tried to create an outline, a good portion of it would be empty.

Many writers get stuck at this point. They may have a great story idea, a few interesting characters, and a plot point or two. They may even be able to write a few scenes in vivid detail. But as soon as they have those scenes down, it all comes to a screeching halt. They simply don't have enough of the story's working parts.

That's where the tarot comes in. In the brainstorming stage, we're creating the characters, scenes, and plot points needed for a viable story. Actually, I think of it more as "uncovering" these things. To me, writing a story has always been like going on an archaeological dig. The story was always there. I just have to dig it out.

So remember: When you're looking at the cards, you're not looking for the whole story—you're looking for its parts. They may be out of order. There may be some things that never even make it into the book. Heck, some of it may be from some bizarro-world alternate reality.

But all of it will make your story better, I promise.

Are You a Pantser or a Plotter?

First, some basic definitions: a "pantser" is someone who doesn't plan their stories before they start writing them (i.e., they "write by the seat of their pants"), and plotters are those who like to plan. Like pretty much anything else, these are two extremes on a spectrum and you might be a little bit of both.

No matter whether you identify as a pantser or a plotter, the tarot can work for you—you'll just be utilizing it at different points in your writing process.

Plotters, you should use the tarot before creating your outline. When we brainstorm with the tarot, we're creating a wealth of ideas that we can draw from. I like to think of it with a garden metaphor: We're fertilizing the soil before we plant the seeds so they'll have all the nutrients and materials necessary to produce healthy blooms and fruit (AKA our stories!).

If you're a pantser, you should use the tarot before you begin writing. Brainstorming with the tarot—especially with some of the structured spreads you'll learn about soon—will help make sure you have all the parts you need for a complete story, even if you don't know when they'll come into play. And don't worry about losing your pantser street cred—you're not really planning, you're just fertilizing the soil your story will grow out of!

The Dos and Don'ts of Reading Tarot for Story Development

Don't be too strict with the card meanings. This is incredibly important. The purpose of using the cards is to spark a creative state—not to bog you down in arbitrary symbolism. The results I get when reading the cards are rarely stellar if I stick too closely to their assigned meanings. What if the cards tell you something that you know in your heart is wrong? Then simply disregard them—the realization that they are wrong is an insight in itself.

Do take notes. It is vital that you have a record of your readings. If I had a paragraph for every amazing story idea I've ever had that I didn't write down because *how could I forget something so obvious and wonderful?*… well, let's just say there aren't enough trees in the world to print all the books I'd have.

Did I mention how important it is to have a tarot journal?

Do deviate from this book. Listen—everything I say in this book is what's worked for me. I hope it will work for you, too. That said, we're all different, and you may find you need to tweak my methods. That's okay. Nothing written here is meant to be taken as gospel. Think of it more as a jumping off point. Keep what works and discard what doesn't.

Do follow a routine. In the introduction to this section, I said that the more often you use the tarot as a creativity tool, the easier it will be. Eventually, it will trigger you to enter a creative "flow" state. The same principle applies to your routine. Listen to the same playlist of music, brainstorm at the same time and in the same place every day, and even drink the same beverage or eat the same snack. Each of these things will signal to your brain, "Hey, it's time to be creative!"

Do be open-minded. The purpose of this book is to teach you to be open to the possibilities in your story. Even if you have an idea of how something in your story should go, let yourself consider alternatives as they occur to you. What if x happened instead of y? You don't have to actually use it, but knowing how your characters would react in different situations means you know them better. You might even find you like the alternative more!

Do devote a time and space to your readings. You'll get the best results from your cards if you give them your complete attention. This isn't something you do with Netflix playing in the background. You want to have a quiet, calm space where you know you won't be interrupted.

You'll also want to devote a set block of time to using the cards. In the past, I've made the mistake of trying to use the cards to brainstorm with the intention of also writing a few thousand words that day. I did this because I didn't want to lose a day of writing. This ended up working *doubly* against me. While I was reading the cards, I felt the pressure to write, so I didn't give them the concentration they deserved. When I sat down to write, I felt guilty about not using the cards right. In the end I lost a whole day of productivity. It's much better to set aside the time. Think of it as an investment.

The Spreads

The rest of the book is devoted to the spreads. A "spread" refers to a shape you lay the cards out in, with each position having an assigned meaning. Each spread is designed with a specific purpose, and each will use a different number of cards. I have separated them into groups based on what aspect of narrative they are for: story prompts, character development, plotting, world building, and writers block. The last section gives tips on creating your own spreads.

Before each spread, I discuss the aspect(s) of narrative theory that it is meant to help with. Each spread includes a diagram, an explanation of each card position, and suggested questions to guide you in your reading.

I used the majority of these spreads while brainstorming my *Pagewalker* and *Jeremiah Jones Cowboy Sorcerer* series. Knowing it might be helpful for you to see real-life examples of readings, I have included several in the text. These came straight from my own tarot journal. I made the decision not to "polish" them, as I wanted their raw nature to show through. Please excuse the stream of consciousness.

To make referring to the spreads easier, I have listed them in a separate section at the end of the book, beginning on page 80. This section includes only the diagram and abbreviated instructions for each. It is also available to download as a printable PDF at www.thewritersaurus.com/tarotdownloads.

Your First Spread

Okay. Got your cards, your journal, and a working pen? Do you have at least a half hour to devote to looking at the cards? If you feel like you can't devote that much time, it's better to come back to it when you do. You're a writer and time is your greatest asset. You can't afford to waste it.

Now go somewhere comfortable and private where you won't be bothered by spouses, kids, or friendly baristas. Seriously, don't go to a coffee shop. You'll just feel self-conscious.

If you'd like, take a few minutes to clear your mind. Meditate, listen to music, or spend some time coloring. I like to knead play dough or silly putty.

Now it's time to get ready for your first spread. Take out your deck, and shuffle the cards. It really doesn't matter how. After you feel they're adequately mixed, cut the deck by dividing it into three stacks, then restacking them in a different order. (In the rest of the book, this step will be called simply, "shuffle and cut your deck.")

Tarot Tip:

As you shuffle, pay attention to any cards that fall out. They may have special insight for your story, so take a few minutes to look up their meanings. You may want to set them aside as you lay out and read the spread.

Now it's time for your first spread. Most spreads use between three and ten cards, though there are spreads that use the entire deck! That's a lot of cards. We'll keep it simple for now—we're going to draw one card.

One-Card Question Spread

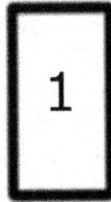

```
┌─────┐
│     │
│  1  │
│     │
└─────┘
```

Answer

From *Tarot for Fiction Writers* - www.thewritersaurus.com

The One-Card Question Spread

It may not seem like a lot, but you'd be surprised how much you can glean from one card. This spread is extremely versatile, and you can use it for just about any purpose. One of the benefits of this spread is that you can be very specific about what you want to know. You also don't have to worry about what the cards mean in relation to each other. Here are some sample questions you might ask:

What is holding my character back?
What are my character's flaws?
What happens at the midpoint of the story?
What is my book's major theme?

You can ask these questions and more, but today we're going to keep it as basic as possible. For your first reading, we're going to ask, *What is my story about?*

Alright. Take out your journal and open to a new page. Write down the date, the story you are reading for, the question you are asking, and the name of the spread.

Now, shuffle and cut your deck, then draw one card and lay it out. It might not make immediate sense. That is okay. Consider the card at face value, its picture, the name, and the number. Is it reversed? What symbols are in the artwork? What's in the background of the picture?

Then, if you need to, refer to the meaning listed in the cheat sheet, and/or the meaning that you wrote down in your journal for that card. Do the keywords have any bearing on the story?

Now, free write your thoughts and insights. It may be beneficial to set a timer. Ten or fifteen minutes is enough. Don't worry if none of it makes sense, or if it doesn't fit together cohesively. Remember—you're just fertilizing your story garden at this point.

What if the card I drew makes no sense? This happens to me all the time. However, when I really apply myself to finding a meaning that works, I end up finding insights and ideas that would have taken me weeks to figure out otherwise, if I would have figured them out at all. One of the reasons we get blocked is that we are in a rut of looking at our story from the same angle. Trying to fit the card in makes us see it from a new perspective. Look at enigmatic spreads as opportunities, because that's what they are.

Help! I came up with a brilliant idea—but it has nothing to do with the meaning of the card! Congratulations! You've unlocked your creativity! You win! If you like the new idea, who cares if it doesn't match the card? The tarot police aren't coming to check on you. A good percentage of the ideas I come up with while reading the cards have nothing to do with the cards themselves. I'm not sure why. I think it has something to do with the seeing the story from a different angle thing I mentioned above.

Example Spread (From My Own Tarot Journal)

This particular spread is from my own tarot journal. I laid it out while brainstorming for my *Pagewalker* series. Remember, these notes aren't refined; they're stream of consciousness writing at times.

Card 1: Six of Pentacles

Example Analysis

The Six of Pentacles, hmmm. Gifts, just rewards, charity. The card seems to indicate cosmic justice, of getting what you deserve, but I don't think that's the message in *Pagewalker,* especially not the first book. It's certainly not charity. April is burdened with the care of the collection, and she's not really given a choice in the matter... but that's not really true, is it? She is given a choice between letting Thaddeus dismantle the library, or protecting it. So I think a more fitting theme is that of doing the right thing and making the best of it. After all, that's what we have to do in real life, right?

Exercise 5: Complete the One-Card Question spread and note it in your tarot journal.

Exercise 6: Make a list of five story-related questions you could ask, then choose one of them and do a reading with it. Note it down in your journal.

Tarot Cards as Story Prompts

Using the tarot to create unique story prompts is an easy and helpful exercise, especially if you are a beginning writer who isn't quite ready to write an entire novel.

Set a timer and do one every day. Not only is it an investment in your writing skills, but it gets you in the habit of writing regularly, which is the most important habit you can cultivate as a writer. I'll bet some of the things you write about will appear in (or at least inform) your future stories.

Tarot Tip:

Any of the spreads listed in this book can be used as writing prompts! Simply lay out the cards and use them to create a story!

One-Card Story Prompt Spread

```
┌─────────┐
│         │
│    1    │
│         │
└─────────┘
```

Prompt

From *Tarot for Fiction Writers* - www.thewritersaurus.com

The One-Card Story Prompt Spread

Does this spread look familiar? Like I said, the one-card spread is extremely versatile. To use it as a story prompt, one option is to ask a question, like in the One-Card Question Spread above, and use the answer as the prompt. You can use any of the questions I listed previously, or one of the questions you wrote for Exercise 6 (because you're totally doing the exercises, right?). Be sure to note the spread name, date, and the card in your tarot journal.

Otherwise, you can simply look at the card's meaning and riff off of that—no need to have a specific question in mind.

Now, set a timer—twenty minutes is good—and start writing on your story prompt. It's not super important that you stick to the prompt, the most important thing is that you write!

Questions:

Can you use the card's keywords in the story?
Consider the card's meaning—is it a situation or character card?

Variation:

Use the illustration depicted on the card is the opening image of your story.

Goal, Motivation, and Conflict Spread

  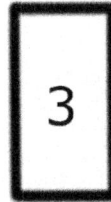

Goal   Motivation   Conflict

From *Tarot for Fiction Writers* - www.thewritersaurus.com

The Goal, Motivation, and Conflict Spread

Shuffle and cut your deck, then lay out three cards in a row. The first card is your character's goal, the second card is what motivates your character to reach that goal, and the third card is what is preventing them from achieving that goal—also known as the story's conflict.

I talk about goals, motivation, and conflict in depth in the "conflict cross" in the next chapter. A great book on writing that addresses this subject is *GMC: Goal, Motivation, and Conflict* by Debra Dixon.

Questions:
What is the relationship between the motivation and the goal?
Is the conflict internal or external?

Variation:
If you'd like, you can add a character card to this spread. Either draw a random card that represents your character or choose one of the figures represented in the illustrations of a card.

Spreads for Character Development

I benefit most from using the tarot for character development. After all, tarot cards are most often used to read people. Why would using the tarot for story development be any different?

When you use the cards as a brainstorming tool, I suggest starting with the characters. They are the most important thing in your story. Plot is important, of course, but it should always be informed by your character's personality and desires. I go over this more in the introduction to the next section.

Following are spreads you can use to develop your characters.

Tarot Tip:

If you haven't already, read the section on character/court cards beginning on page 122. I explain several concepts there that you will need to know to get the most benefit out of the spreads in this section.

The Importance of Motivation

There are many facets to character creation, including physical appearance, origin, backstory, likes and dislikes, and more. You probably realize the importance of having a goal for your character. But do you know that your character *also* needs to have a personal motivation for that goal? Otherwise, what keeps them from giving up when the going gets tough?

Still, it is common to see a character following a goal without any motivation at all. A problem shows up, and they decide to tackle it, apparently for kicks and giggles. Perhaps just as common is the character who goes after a goal because it is "the right thing," or because they are the good guy and that is what good guys do. The problem with that is that if they fail, there is no skin off their teeth—things for them won't change, no matter how bad they feel.

So what makes a good motivation? Well, here is a list of common types, though it is by no means exhaustive. Notice that each one implies personal stakes for the character:

Vengeance: The antagonist has wronged them (or someone they love) in some way. The character is hell-bent on righting this wrong.

Example: In *The Princess Bride,* Inigo Montoya has waited his entire life to find Count Rugen, the man that murdered his father, and kill him.

To Save Themselves: If they don't achieve their goal, the character will face dire consequences, maybe even death.

Example: In *Storm's Edge,* the first book in the Dresden Files series, Henry Dresden must find the real killer, or the White Council will believe he committed the crimes and execute him.

To Save Someone Else: The character needs to achieve their goal in order to save someone they deeply care about.

Example: In *The Hunger Games,* Katniss volunteers as tribute in order to save her sister.

To Prove Themselves: The character must achieve their goal in order to prove that they are worthy of something.

Example: In *The Silence of the Lambs,* Clarice Starling wants to prove her capabilities as an agent.

To Gain Something: If the character achieves their goal, they gain something, maybe money, maybe power. Whatever it is, gaining it will have a direct effect on their life—perhaps a member of their family is sick, and they don't have enough money to pay for treatment. It's important to have these special stakes if the goal is money, as otherwise if they fail, things just go back to the way they were.

Example: In *Charlie and the Chocolate Factory,* the Buckets' lives will change immensely with the lifetime supply of chocolate. In *Storm's Edge,* Harry Dresden must solve the case in order to get paid and pay his rent.

Note that some of these goals lasted the entire book or movie, even an entire series, while others lasted only a scene. Goals can be resolved within a story—but they must be immediately replaced by another goal, or the reader will stop reading. It's a good idea to repeat the Character Cross spread at this point.

Also note that not all of these goals are life and death. Sometimes it's enough for your character to need to pay his rent. Just remember, the goal has to be worth the pain and strife the character must go through to achieve it. Otherwise, why wouldn't they just give up?

The Importance of Conflict

Conflict is what keeps your character from achieving a goal. Without a conflict, there is no story, because the character can achieve their goal with no problem.

There are seven common types of conflict. You probably remember them from high school English class:

Character vs. Character: The character must overcome the efforts of an antagonist (or group of antagonists) to achieve their goal. This is probably the most common type of conflict. It's important to remember that the antagonist(s) must also have a goal. Just as many writers make the mistake of having their protagonists go after a goal because "it's the right thing," many more have their antagonists commit atrocious acts simply because they're the bad guys, or they're obsessed with foiling the hero. An example is Bluto in the Popeye comics and cartoon. In a character vs. character conflict, it's important that **both** the protagonist and antagonist have motivated goals. **The success of those goals must be mutually exclusive.** That means for the hero to achieve their goal, the antagonist must fail to achieve theirs, and vice versa. There can be no "everyone wins" situations here, no loopholes.

Example: In *The Lord of the Rings,* Frodo's goal is to destroy the ring, while Sauron's goal is to use it to gain power. If one succeeds, the other fails.

Character vs. Nature: The thing that stops the character from achieving their goal is nature, perhaps a sudden ice age, freak superstorm, or massive tornado. Most often, the character's goal in these types of stories is just to survive.

Example: In *The Day After Tomorrow,* the characters must survive a cataclysmic climate shift.

Character vs. Society: The character's opponent is society at large. They see wrong in the way society acts, and they want to change it—but society never likes to be changed. Those in power come after the protagonist.

Example: In the third Hunger Games book, Katniss joins a band of rebels to fight the capitol's reign of terror over the districts. Other stories with a character vs. society conflict include *The Giver, Divergent,* and *The Maze Runner.*

Character vs. Self: What prevents the character from reaching their goal is their own fears, attitudes, or inability to change. This form of conflict is often the most difficult to pin down, and usually requires a separate external conflict. It's important to note that almost all stories will have some internal conflict (character vs. self) that must be overcome to achieve their goal. Stories where character vs. self is the most prominent form of conflict present are often downfall stories, where the character goes from being good to being bad.

Example: In the Harry Potter books, Harry is often afraid that he is a dark wizard just like Voldemort. In *Lord of the Rings,* Frodo must fight his desire to possess the ring. In seasons 5-7 of *Buffy the Vampire Slayer,* Spike must wrestle with his inner monster to finally become one of the good guys.

Character vs. Technology: The force that prevents the character from achieving their goal is technological.

Example: In *The Terminator* franchise, the characters must face cyborgs from the future to prevent them from taking over the world.

Character vs. Supernatural: This form of conflict is often not included in the "five forms of literary conflict," but I'm including it here in favor of thoroughness. This is where the character must overcome a supernatural force of some sort. It is often the conflict in horror stories.

Example: In *The Exorcist,* the protagonists must band together to save a girl who is being possessed by a demon.

It's important to note that most stories have instances of more than one of these conflict types. The exception to this rule is very short stories.

Character Cross Spread

```
                        ┌─────┐
                        │     │
                        │  5  │
                        │     │
                        └─────┘
                         Goal

┌─────┐           ┌───────────┐          ┌─────┐
│     │         ┌─┤           ├─┐        │     │
│  4  │         │ │     2     │ │  ⊥     │  6  │
│     │         │ │           │ │  ⊂     │     │
└─────┘         └─┤           ├─┘  o      └─────┘
                  │           │    n
 Need             └───────────┘    f       Want
                   Character        l
                                    i
                                    c
                                    t

                        ┌─────┐
                        │     │
                        │  3  │
                        │     │
                        └─────┘
                        flaws
```

From *Tarot for Fiction Writers*
www.thewritersaurus.com

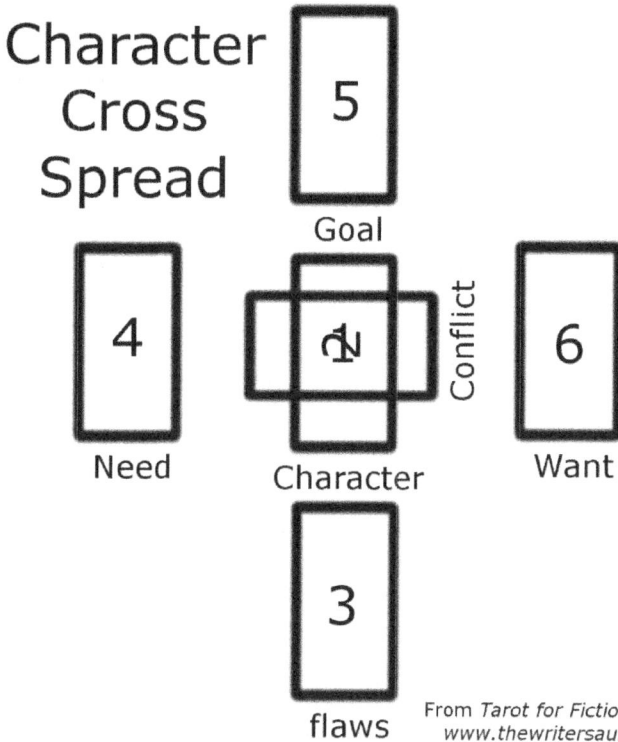

The Character Cross Spread

The Character Cross spread deals with your character's motivations and goals. It gives a general reading for a character in the present, either at the beginning of your story, or at a point in the story where the character's goals and/or motivation change.

Shuffle and cut your deck, then lay out six cards in the positions in the graphic above. The main character card is in the center, the goal card directly above them, the external conflict card crossing over them horizontally. To their left is their need, to their right is their want. The need card and the want card make up the character's motivation. Note that the need and want can sometimes be in harmony with each other, but often they are in opposition, and the character needs to overcome that dichotomy somehow. This is especially true for character vs. self conflict. Below the character is a card representing that character's internal conflict.

Questions:
Are my character's want and need in harmony or opposition? What effect does this have on the story overall?
Are there any similarities between the internal conflict and external conflict?
Which of the five types is the external conflict?

Example Spread (From My Own Tarot Journal)
I chose to do this spread for Jeremiah Jones, the main character of my weird west serial, *Jeremiah Jones Cowboy Sorcerer*. Though I already finished the first season of this serial, I felt like I needed more insight in Jeremiah's motivation going into the second season.
Card 1: Reversed Knight of Swords
Card 2: Three of Wands
Card 3: Reversed Ten of Cups
Card 4: Reversed Ten of Swords
Card 5: The Devil
Card 6: The Hanged Man

Example Analysis
Jeremiah is represented by the reversed Knight of Swords, indicating his tendency to float through life with little agency. The Three of Wands in the conflict card position represents the circle wanting what he has and thinking they have a right to it. The Ten of Cups indicates Jay's need for a stable, loving home with people who accept him. The devil card in the want position may indicate that what Jay thinks he needs/wants is actually holding him back. The reversed Ten of Swords points to the death of his father, indicating that one of Jay's goals throughout season two is to find out who killed his father.

A Note on Villains and Motivation
If your book happens to be of the character vs. character variety, that means that you have an antagonist. Some people may refer to that antagonist as a villain.

I personally don't like the word villain. It makes it too easy to create the type of "bad for the sake of being bad" guy mentioned briefly above, a Dastard Dan who ties the maiden to the railroad tracks just because he can, motivation be damned.

There are certain types of stories where this works. The recent glut of superhero movies is a good example—all of them have super-sized, vaguely demonic gods bent on destruction for… reasons, I guess? Despite this flaw, these movies remain popular. But they could be a lot better if the villains were more developed.

There are a lot more where it doesn't work. Novice writers fall back on this stereotype because it's easier. It's *hard* to give a villain believable motivation. If the mean girl at school is a bitch because she's being abused at home, or the mad scientist is kidnapping and experimenting on people in order to find a cure for her terminally ill husband, well, that complicates things a little bit. You/the reader probably sympathize with the villain. Heck, maybe you'd even do the same thing in that situation.

Even more complicated is if the antagonist is actually *right*. Maybe his methods are off, but his reasoning is sound. The things he does are at least a little understandable. The protagonist is more right, of course (at least for the purposes of the story being told), but that doesn't mean the villain isn't also right.

This is what turns your antagonist from a cardboard cutout of a character and into someone who feels real. Not only that, but it will make your readers uncomfortable, because they can't say for sure which character is right. This discomfort will make them want to read until the end to see what happens.

An example of a well-motivated, arguably right antagonist is Magneto from the X-Men comics and films. While Charles Xavier and the X-men fight to protect the humans that fear them, Magneto wants mutants to band together before humanity is able to commit mutant genocide. This is informed by Magneto's time in a German concentration camp during WWII.

Exercise 7: Take out your notes and write down your antagonist's motivation. If they don't have one, lay out the conflict cross spread for them. Try to see the situation from their perspective. In their head, they should be the hero.

All about the Backstory

Backstory is a tricky thing. Your character needs at least a little of it, otherwise they won't feel real, but it's really easy to overdo it and get world builder's disease. World builder's disease is where you keep developing your world when you should be writing your story—but more on that when we talk about world building.

Only you can decide when you have enough backstory. I tend towards having less backstory when I start writing. Anyway, I always end up learning about my characters as I draft. Having too much backstory when you start may also impede your narrative rather than help it.

Backstory Spread

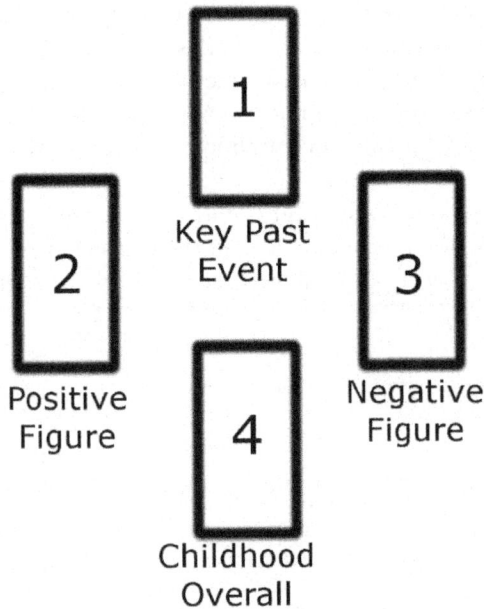

	1	
2	**Key Past Event**	**3**
Positive Figure	**4**	**Negative Figure**
	Childhood Overall	

From *Tarot for Fiction Writers* - www.thewritersaurus.com

The Backstory Spread

This spread includes a card for a key event in the character's life, the person who's had the most positive impact on them, the person who's had the most negative impact on them, and a card representing their early life overall.

Keep in mind that most of what you uncover while looking at this spread will not appear in the book at all—but it will inform it. The exception is if there is a relationship between the present problem and something that happened in the past. For example, let's say a character failed in a situation when they were younger, and they face a similar situation in the present. That is something you'll want to highlight, because it raises the emotional stakes.

An example is from the 2004 movie *Miracle on Ice*. The movie opens on the lead character, Herb Brooks, when he was a child. A hockey game has gone into overtime. Herb is out on the ice, alone except for the opposing team's goalie. All he has to do is get the puck in the net, and his team will win the game. He skates, he shoots—and the puck bounces off of the net's frame. Herb falls to his knees and hangs his head as the opposing team gathers to celebrate. We see a stern coach give Herb a look of disappointment.

This scene informs the rest of the movie, especially the final scene. We see brief flashes of it throughout the narrative—yet it is incredibly short.

Questions:

Are there any relationships or foils between the spreads?
What links are there with the present story conflict?
Do either of the important characters appear in the current story?

Example Spread (From My Own Tarot Journal)

I did this spread for Sam, one of the characters in *Jeremiah Jones Cowboy Sorcerer.*

Card 1: Reversed World
Card 2: King of Pentacles
Card 3: Judgement
Card 4: Reversed Hermit

Example Analysis

Sam is a mixed-race wizard born to a voodoo priestess and a wizard plantation owner. The reversed World represents how Sam grew up in an affluent family, but it still wasn't enough, because she never felt like either of her upbringings really belonged to her. As I puzzled over the King of Pentacles and Judgement cards, I knew they represented her parents. It came to me that both were negative and positive forces in her life. If that weren't the case, she would have been more married to one of her identities. The Reversed Hermit represents how she felt isolated from her peers. It was because of this isolation that she started reading a lot of books, which led to her love of knowledge and her current role in the Havenites.

A few things became clear to me tangential to the cards, and I wanted to share them with you so that you could see how much a tarot spread can unearth. The following is all backstory that "came to me" as I read this spread. It's a good example of how tarot can spark creativity beyond the meanings of the cards themselves. Sam's mother lived in New Orleans, where her father lived for several months, either on vacation or perhaps for school or business. Her mother had a harsh life, but she survived it all and became a figure of immense power. I can see that when they met, she saw Sam's father and said, "There is power in you," or something similar, which was the beginning of their affair. I also see that Sam had a tutor that nurtured her intelligence. This tutor was very superstitious. He saw something happen as Sam's magic emerged, and he was afraid of her and quit the next day. Knowing this background information allows me to write Sam's character in a more consistent and specific way—she is motivated by her history and her background and she's become a stronger character in the story because of this.

The Importance of Relationships

Relationships between characters may be the most compelling aspect of storytelling, but it is one that is often overlooked. We spend days, weeks, or months (if we're plotters) developing bad-ass, interesting characters and crafting twisting, unpredictable plots. Those are both important things. But what makes us return to our favorite books, television shows, and movies again and again?

The relationships, of course, and not just the romantic ones. The plot and character development might be what draws readers in, but it's the relationships between the characters that make them want to keep reading—and maybe even pick up the next book in the series!

For example, what kept me watching through season five of *Buffy the Vampire Slayer* (arguably not the best season) was the relationship between Spike and Buffy. Even though it hadn't gotten to the self-destructive romantic phase yet, I wanted to know if Buffy would give Spike a chance, and if his obsession with her would make transform him from the monster he was into something else.

The **Key Relationships Spread** will help you pinpoint three important relationships that your character has. They may be past friendships, formative relationships, romantic, or destructive. One important one to look out for is their relationship with the antagonist.

Key
Relationships
Spread

┌───┐
│ 3 │
└───┘
C

MC = main character
C = character
R = relationship

┌───┐
│ 6 │
└───┘
R

┌───┐ ┌───┐ ┌───┐ ┌───┐ ┌───┐
│ 4 │ │ 7 │ │ 1 │ │ 5 │ │ 2 │
└───┘ └───┘ └───┘ └───┘ └───┘
  C   R   MC   R   C

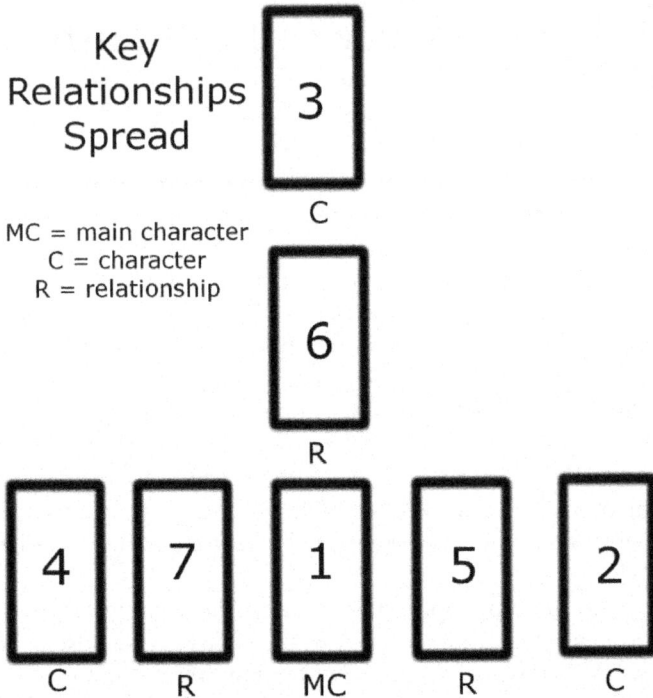

From *Tarot for Fiction Writers - www.thewritersaurus.com*

The Key Relationships Spread

For this one, you'll want to separate out the sixteen court cards. (For more info on the court cards and how they relate to character, refer to the section on character cards on page 122.) This is your character deck. Choose a card representing your character based on their characteristics. Set this in the middle of the spread in the 1 position. Then shuffle the character deck. Draw three more character cards in positions 2, 3, and 4, leaving space between each card and the hero card.

Now, shuffle the remaining deck. Place cards in the 5, 6, and 7 positions. These cards represent the relationship between the hero and the other characters. How they represent the relationship is yours to interpret. It may be an experience they shared, how they generally relate to each other, or a goal they have in common. Is the card in the same suit as your character? That may show a family member or a friend.

Watch out for foils!

If one of the character cards you draw has the same court position as your hero (for example, both are knights or both are queens) you may consider whether or not that character is a foil of the hero. A foil is someone who is either very similar to your character, or the polar opposite of them. They were put in a similar situation as our hero, but made different choices. This is an opportunity to highlight where your character could be now if they had done things a little differently.

Questions:
Which of these relationships are positive? Which are negative?
Are any of the character cards in the same suit?
Are all of these characters currently in the main character's life?

Tarot Tip:
When I do spreads like this that deal with character, I lay out only the character cards at first. For The Key Relationships Spread, that's cards 1-4. I read those cards, and once I feel I understand them, I lay out the rest of the cards. That way it's not as overwhelming!

Example Spread (From My Own Tarot Journal)
I decided to do this spread for my next project, *Pagewalker.*

Card 1: Reversed Knight of Cups (chosen to represent the main character's stagnation and indecision)
Card 2: Queen of Swords
Card 3: King of Wands
Card 4: Reversed King of Swords
Card 5: Death
Card 6: Ace of Cups
Card 7: Reversed Three of Wands

Example Analysis
The Queen of Swords represents Mae, the former Pagewalker, and the one who hired April at the library. The Death card represents her actual death (which is rare for the death card—it usually represents the end of something rather than literal passing away.) It may also represent Mae's role as the Pagewalker ending so that April's role can begin. The defining role that Mae will take in April's life is that she died too soon to teach April about being a Pagewalker.

On the other side, we have the Reversed King of Swords, which represents the first season antagonist, Thaddeus. It is fitting that he and Mae both are represented by Sword cards, as they are foils of each other—both *to* each other, and in their roles in April's life. The Knight card is reversed because, while Thaddeus thinks he is working for the right side, he's actually been deceived—the things he thinks are true really aren't.

On top we have the King of Wands, which represents April's relationship with Randall. The Ace of Cups show that Randall is the person who April will be closest to.

One-on-One
Relationship Spread

C1 = character 1
C2 = character 2
R = relationship

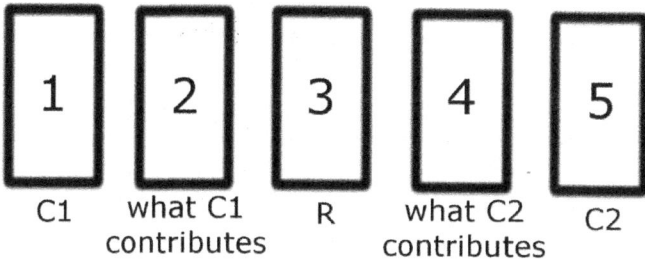

1	2	3	4	5
C1	what C1 contributes	R	what C2 contributes	C2

From *Tarot for Fiction Writers - www.thewritersaurus.com*

The One-on-One Relationship Spread

This is another spread that can help you discover more about the relationships between your characters. As the name suggests, this spread deals with a single relationship between two characters. You can use this spread for any characters that interact on a regular basis, but I find it especially helpful to do this spread between two characters who don't meet often. *Buffy the Vampire Slayer* does this masterfully. We expect Spike to interact with Buffy and the other scoobies... what's unexpected is the relationship formed between Spike and Buffy's mom, Joyce, over daytime soap operas. These unexpected connections allow us to explore and develop our characters in a myriad of interesting ways.

To do this spread, separate out your character cards from the deck and shuffle them. Draw two and place them in the 1 and 2 positions. These cards represent the two characters. They should be drawn and not selected, as we're trying to discover who our characters are in in the relationship—we already know who they are in the overall story. Draw the rest of the cards from the remaining trump/number cards deck. Card 3 represents what character 1 contributes to the relationship, and card 4 represents what character 2 brings to the relationship. Card 5 represents the overall relationship.

Example Spread (From My Own Tarot Journal)

I used this spread for two of the main characters in my *Pagewalker* series, April and Randall.

Card 1: Reversed Queen of Pentacles
Card 2: King of Pentacles
Card 3: Reversed Wands
Card 4: Two of Wands
Card 5: Reversed Strength

Example Analysis

The first thing I noticed was that both character cards were Pentacles, meaning they're both on the same team, and of the same philosophy. It feels right that Randall would be the Knight to April's Queen, because he is her right-hand man, her most trusted advisor, and her protector. The Queen of Pentacles is reversed because Randall is the only one April shows her insecurities and doubts to. The World card is reversed because she is not sure how she will complete her mission. The fact that the strength card was reversed flummoxed me for a while—friends are stronger when they're together, after all. But then I realized: Their strength when they're together and their reliance on one-another (particularly April's reliance on Randall) also makes them each other's weakness. I knew, suddenly, that Randall would be kidnapped at some point in the series to force April's hand.

The Five-Man Band

We know that relationships between characters are important, but what about the group dynamic? Enter the five-man band.

The five-man band is a trope that describes the dynamics of a group, and what each person in the group contributes. Why do we need the five-man band? For three reasons. The first is that we want to have the needs of the group met—if you have five super-strong warrior-types, that might be really awesome for fight scenes, but what about when logic and knowledge are needed? Then your group would really be in a pickle.

The second reason is that we want to make sure the reader remembers all of your characters. One of the ways to do that is to give each character their own purpose. That way, when a character is mentioned again, the reader will think, *Oh, yeah—this guy is the really smart person who is always doing mathematical calculations in that notepad they keep in their pocket.*

The third reason is that we want each character to have a purpose in the narrative. Otherwise they might as well not be in the story. (Fiction is a dog-eat-dog world, my friends.)

But **What is the Five-Man Band?**

The five-man band can be broken into five roles, each corresponding to a suit of the tarot:

The Hero: Pretty self-explanatory. This is our main character, the leader of the group. While the other members of the five-man band each have their purpose and role to play, the will be at odds without the hero to direct them. The Hero is represented by the Major Arcana.

The Lancer: The Lancer is the hero's right-hand man (or woman), his best friend. They will advocate for the hero when he is not around, and they will take his place as leader when the hero has to be elsewhere. The Lancer is represented by the suit of Wands.

The Smart Guy: The Smart Guy is the one with the knowledge. They are a researcher, a scientist, a librarian, or something equivalent. They find the information the others need to do their jobs. The corresponding suit is Swords.

The Tough Guy: The Tough Guy, or The Big Guy, as he (or she) is sometimes known, is just that. They're the muscle, the intimidator, the one who gets things done. They may sometimes be simple-minded, in contrast to The Smart Guy. The corresponding suit is the suit of Pentacles.

The Heart: The Heart is the emotional core of the group. They bring everyone together. Traditionally, this role has been referred to as "The Chick" (The popular website tvtropes.com even goes as far as to say that if the role isn't filled by a woman then it isn't a five-man band), but us savvy writers know that any of the above roles can be filled by either sex.

So that's the five-man band.

But isn't that boring and formulaic?

Yes and no. The five-man band is a starting point, a form that makes sure you've filled all the roles your story needs and that each member is distinct and memorable… but if you stick to it too closely, you'll end up with one-dimensional characters. Snooze-fest!

One thing a formula or trope like the five-man band does is give us expectations that we can **subvert**. **Subversion** is where we buck reader expectations. The Tough Guy has an unexpected love for cooking (As Lance, the "tough guy" from *Jeremiah Jones Cowboy Sorcerer* does), the Smart Guy may be dyslexic, and The Heart may have a mouth like a sailor.

Another trick you can use is to have your characters fill different roles depending on the problem. For example, in *Buffy the Vampire,* Willow and Giles share the roles of Lancer and Smart Guy. If the research needed is arcane, Giles will be The Smart Guy and Willow The Lancer, but if the problem is technological or Witchcraft-oriented, then their positions switch. Cool, huh?

Five-Man Band Spread

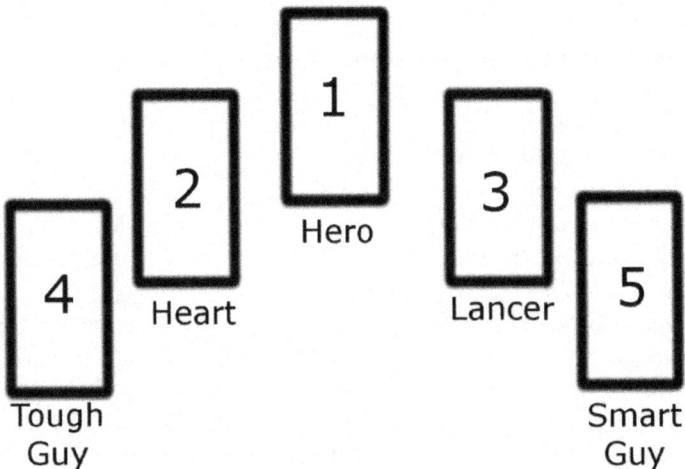

From *Tarot for Fiction Writers* - www.thewritersaurus.com

The Five Man Band Spread

If your court cards are still separated out, take a few minutes to mix them back in. We need the deck whole for this one.

Draw five cards and arrange them in an arrow formation as shown in the diagram.

Card 1 represents The Hero. The Heart and The Lancer are both next to the hero, The Heart on the left (Card 2) and The Lancer on the right (Card 3). Behind The Heart on the left is The Tough Guy (Card 4), and behind The Lancer on the right is The Smart Guy (Card 5).

Tarot Tip:

Look for relationships between the cards—does The Lancer have a beef with The Smart Guy? Does The Tough Guy have a crush on The Heart? These could be possible sub-plots in your story.

Questions:

Do any of the band members serve as foils to the hero?

Are there any interesting similarities between any of the members?

Do any court cards appear? These may indicate close relationships between band members of that suit, or perhaps unresolved issues.

Five-Man Band Spread

(Variation)

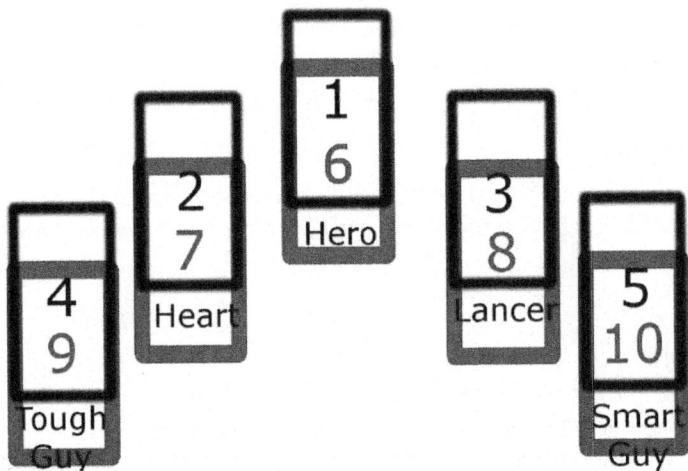

From *Tarot for Fiction Writers* - www.thewritersaurus.com

Five-Man Band Spread Variation:

Lay out cards 1-5 per the directions for the Five-Man Band Spread. After you have finished your reading for this layer, lay out five more cards—one on top of each character card as shown by the blue in the above diagram.

Each of these cards represents a secondary character trait for the character it modifies. This helps us flesh them out and make them interesting. Remember, we don't want any one-dimensional characters!

Variation Questions:

Is each character's secondary interest in harmony with their primary role, or is it at odds with it? What does this add to the story?

Are there similarities between one character's primary role and another's secondary interest? This may show that that character would rather serve in that role. This could be a source of conflict or character growth.

Example Spread (From My Own Tarot Journal)

I used the variation on The Five-Man Band Spread to do a reading for the characters from *Jeremiah Jones Cowboy Sorcerer*. Though that series is partially an ensemble piece, the characters cannot be easily divided into the roles listed above. One reason for this is that I have six characters, not five, with two characters swapping the hero position. I decided to give it a go, anyway.

I laid out and read the character cards first, then added the secondary trait cards.

Card 1: Page of Wands
Card 2: Reversed Knight of Cups
Card 3: Seven of Cups
Card 4: Queen of Wands
Card 5: Six of Wands
Card 6: Reversed Nine of Swords
Card 7: The Tower
Card 8: Four of Wands
Card 9: Reversed Lovers
Card 10: Five of Wands

Example Analysis

There are a lot of Wands and Cups, here, which points to a lot of emotion, passion, and work ethic.

Pentacle of Wands in the hero position.... Hmm. Does this refer to Jesse or Jeremiah? Or perhaps both of them? Jesse is more of a doer. The Reversed Nine of Swords as the secondary trait card also points to Jesse's mental issues he's been having after coming back from the dead.

The Knight of Cups in The Heart position. I have Heather as The Heart. Though I haven't written about it yet, Heather's ultimate destiny is to go back to her pack and end the misogyny and totalitarianism there. Perhaps the thread that ultimately brings her back there starts in season two?

I decided to have George be The Lancer, though if Jesse were the Hero, then Jeremiah would be The Lancer. The Seven of Cups points to creativity and invention, the perfect card for a tinker. This card tells me that George needs to be careful not to get lost in his own head. The Reversed Four of Wands could augment that. Maybe this is one of the reasons George and Sam have so many marital troubles.

For this spread, Lance is The Tough Guy, which makes the Queen of Swords an interesting card for him, especially in the five-man band spread. However, it is accurate—Lance is passionate, and more nurturing than he lets on when you first get to know him. He loves cooking, and goes to the Youth Center regularly to teach Home Ec to the kids there. Perhaps he had a female mentor who taught him to use his runes, since he stole them?

Sam is The Smart Guy, of course. The Six of Wands is a victory card. Perhaps her knowledge and insight is always the key to the Havenite's victory... maybe one that the others don't show enough appreciation for.

Beyond the cards, I see that George and Sam met while George was attempting to steal a very dangerous artefact from Sam's father. Prequel material!

The Power Trio

As useful as the five-man band is, some stories simply don't have a lot of characters. Enter the power trio. A power trio is comprised of three characters, the hero and two companions. It's often broken down into the hero, the hero's best friend, and the hero's love interest.

Each of these three characters represents one of Aristotle's three modes of persuasion: ethos, pathos, and logos. Ethos refers to the ethical manner of persuasion and is concerned with morality and right or wrong. That's our hero. One of the hero's companions will represent pathos, or emotion. The other will represent logos, or logic.

The most famous power trio is undoubtedly Harry, Ron, and Hermione from *Harry Potter*. Harry is ethos, Ron is pathos, and Hermione is logos.

But why do I need all three? you might ask. Why can't I have two logos characters, or two pathos characters? Well, fiction is about conflict, even amongst the "good guys." Logos and pathos are always at odds—one errs on the side of doing what is logical, the other on what feels right. Both can be right or wrong at different times, and sometimes even simultaneously. The ethos character balances these two extremes. In fact, part of the hero's job is to mediate between these two friends, to focus them on a common goal.

As with the five-man band, it's important to not be too rigid about the roles, and to even let the characters switch from time to time. To draw from the *Harry Potter* example, Harry, Ron, and Hermione are all smart, ethical, and emotional—each just embodies one of those traits a little more than the others.

One example of a power trio done incorrectly is, funny enough, the Harry Potter movie adaptations. In the books, Ron always keeps his cool in stressful situations (unless spiders are involved, of course) while Hermione tends to panic. One example is in a scene from the first book where Ron is caught in the devil's snare. Hermione correctly remembers that the plant doesn't like heat, but is so panicked that she can't remember how to apply this knowledge—her weakness is her emotion. It's Ron who keeps his cool and reminds her that she can light a fire using magic. Compare that to the same scene in the movie, where Ron is panicked and yelling, and Hermione immediately remembers the solution and executes it.

If you go through and compare the movies to the books, it's pretty clear that it was a conscious choice to take the moments that demonstrated Ron's emotional capability and give them instead to Hermione, often nearly word-for-word or action-for-action. I have linked to a couple videos that give examples of this in the resources section.

This is detrimental to the story in two ways. First, it takes away Hermione's flaws, making her a "perfect" character. Second, it robs Ron of his strengths and turns him into nothing more than comic relief. This weakens the power trio and begs the question of why Ron is there at all—remember, we have to NEED each character in the power trio!

Power Trio Spread

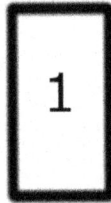

1

ethos character
(hero)

2

logos
character

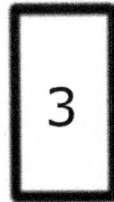

3

pathos
character

From *Tarot for Fiction Writers* - www.thewritersaurus.com

The Power Trio Spread

Separate out your court cards again. Draw three court cards and place them in the shape of a triangle as you see in the diagram. Then draw three cards from the trump/number deck, placing one on each of the triangle's legs. Then place a final trump/number card in the middle of the triangle.

The court cards in the corners each represent a member of the Power Trio. The card on the top point is the hero (ethos), the card on the right point is logos, and the card on the left point is pathos.

Questions:

Are the logos and pathos characters in harmony, or are they at odds? Does this externalize an internal conflict in the ethos character?

Which of these characters in the group is the weakest? Could an antagonist use these weakness against the group?

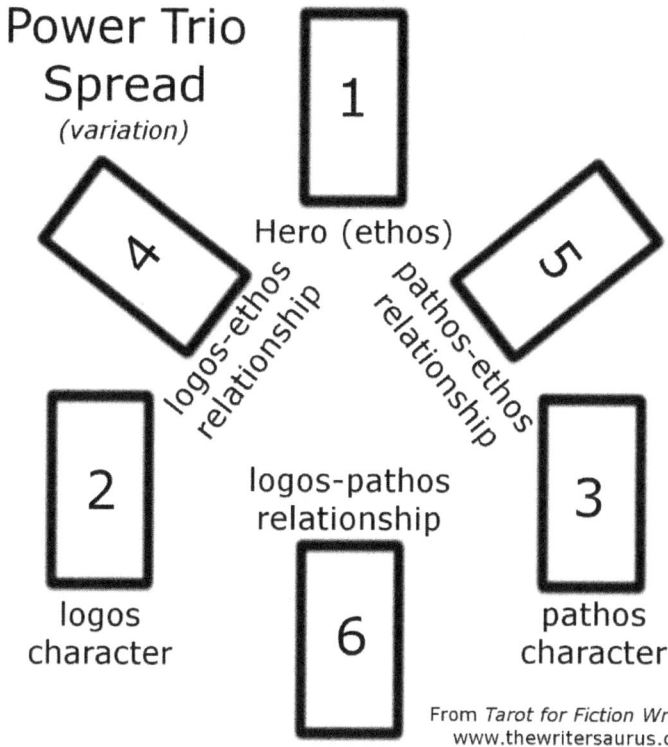

Power Trio Spread
(variation)

1

4

Hero (ethos)

5

logos-ethos relationship

pathos-ethos relationship

2

logos-pathos relationship

3

logos character

6

pathos character

From *Tarot for Fiction Writers* -
www.thewritersaurus.com

Variation

Lay out and read cards 1-3 per the instructions for the Power Trio Spread. Then lay out a card from the non-court deck between each of these cards as shown in the diagram above. Each of these cards represents the relationship of the characters it's sitting between.

Variation Questions

Of all the bonds in the trio, which is the strongest?
Which bond is the weakest? This could be a point of dissention in the trio.

Example Spread (From My Own Tarot Journal)

This example spread again comes from *Pagewalkers*. I already have three main characters who can form a Power Trio, but apart from the ethos role, I'm not sure which role the other two will take.

Card 1: Seven of Swords
Card 2: Ace of Pentacles
Card 3: Reversed Eight of Pentacles
Card 4: Queen of Cups

Card 5: Ace of Swords
Card 6: Seven of Wands

Example Analysis

I laid out the character cards (1-3) first. The Ace of Pentacles seems to point to Randall's stability as a part of the trio, which is in direct conflict with his PTSD and the fact that he is homeless.

The Reversed Eight of Pentacles means that Dorian is now April's mentor in the ways of the Pagewalker, the same as Mae was his mentor in overcoming his vices.

The Seven of Swords was a hard card to read at first, because it refers to dishonesty and thievery. It didn't seem to fit with April's personality. It refers to her imposter syndrome. Maybe she feels like she isn't fit to be the Pagewalker, or lead Dorian and Randall, who she feels have more experience than she does.

After I was satisfied with my understanding of the character cards, I laid out the relationship cards. The Ace of Swords between Dorian and April solidifies his role as her teacher.

The Seven of Wands points to Dorian and Randall's contentious relationship, but also the fact that they'll have each other's back in a fight.

The Queen of Cups refers to Randall and April's eventual familial relationship. He becomes like a father to her.

I also placed a card (Page of Cups) in the center of the triangle to represent the trio as a whole. The Page of Cups refers to the trio eventually forming strong, emotional bonds. Will April one day have to choose between them?

The Tarot and Plot

Following are several spreads to help you develop your story's plot. Like the section on character, each spread is prefaced by an explanation of why its elements are so important.

Most of these spreads are based on common plot structures and have more shape than the spreads for character. Even so, I find that doing readings for plot is not as intuitive as reading for character, especially in the beginning. I found that much of the insight I was getting was still about character. If you have the same issue, that's fine. Character and plot are heavily linked, as I will explain in the next section.

Its very unlikely that any of these readings will immediately illuminate an entire scene or plot point. Instead, they will often show you a single element, like the beam of a flashlight in a dark room. It's your job to relate that element to a larger plot, either through your own creativity or by laying out another spread.

As stated earlier, don't try to judge everything yet. Just take notes. Something that doesn't make sense now may make sense later.

A Rant on Character-Driven vs. Plot-Driven Stories

I'm a member of a lot of writing groups on Facebook, and every so often I'll see a post about "character vs. plot-driven" novels and stories. The comment section is always filled with support for one or another—the favorite answer is, by far, character-driven. There seems to be a stigma for plot-driven works. I can understand this, because it's the reader's connection to the characters that keeps them interested. Even those who say they their books are driven primarily by plot are the first to say that the books they're writing aren't literary masterpieces.

I always find professing your allegiance to one or the other strange. I also feel it reveals a bit of ignorance. Character and plot are inextricably tied together by thousands of tiny strings. If one moves, the rest move along with it.

When done correctly, plot is shaped by a character, and in time, your protagonist will be shaped by the plot—this is called a character arc. To say that one is better than the other is ludicrous. Plot is not just a series of events happening to a certain character—it's a series of events happening to a character in a personal way, and the character acting and reacting in accordance.

Let's take the example of *The Hunger Games*. In the reaping scene, Katniss volunteers to take her sister's place in the games. We know from an earlier scene that protecting and caring for her sister is something that is deeply important to Katniss. Without this character attribute, Katniss would not have ended up in the games and we wouldn't have our story.

Some might argue that Katniss' name could have been drawn outright, but it wouldn't have the same emotional punch. The reader wouldn't sympathize with Katniss as much (this is the "save the cat" moment for students of Blake Snyder), and would be in danger of putting the book down in favor of more cathartic entertainment—as I said above, it's the reader's attachment to the characters that keeps them interested. Rue's death later in the book, and Katniss' reaction to it, wouldn't have the same effect and meaning. In fact, without that motivation, the course of the story might have taken a completely different turn.

Plot and character are linked, and neither is more important than the other.

Tarot Tip:

You can use the spreads that follow while brainstorming to generate or uncover the parts of your story. You can also use them as frame works while outlining. Having a visual representation of the story's structure can make the outlining process easier and the resulting story more cohesive. To use this method, lay out cards in the structure you want to follow. You may use cards that are representative of the story's events, or random cards, whichever works best for you. Refer to them as needed.

The Tarot and the Hero's Journey

The hero's journey is one of the most popular plot templates. It was first detailed in Joseph Campbell's book *The Hero with a Thousand Faces*. Campbell had studied hundreds of stories from different cultures and found that most myths have the same basic structure. In *The Hero with a Thousand Faces* he referred to this as the "monomyth," but it is better known as "the hero's journey." Though Campbell never intended it to be used as a structure for writers, that is what is has become.

I've never intentionally used the hero's journey to plan out my books, though most of them adhere to the concept at least in part. Someday when I have more time I might sit down and try to map one and see how well it conforms. It's my suspicion that while a few stories may map exactly, most only truly adhere to the structure in parts—and that's not a bad thing. It means we can use the parts that best suit our purposes and fudge the rest.

That said, this book wouldn't be complete without including at least one spread for the hero's journey. Following is a spread that will help you look at your plot in its entirety. If you want a more in-depth look at the hero's journey through the tarot, check out Arwen Lynch's *Mapping the Hero's Journey with Tarot: 33 Days to Finish Your Novel*. She goes through the structure step-by-step and has a spread for each of the twelve phases of the hero's journey.

Hero's Journey Spread

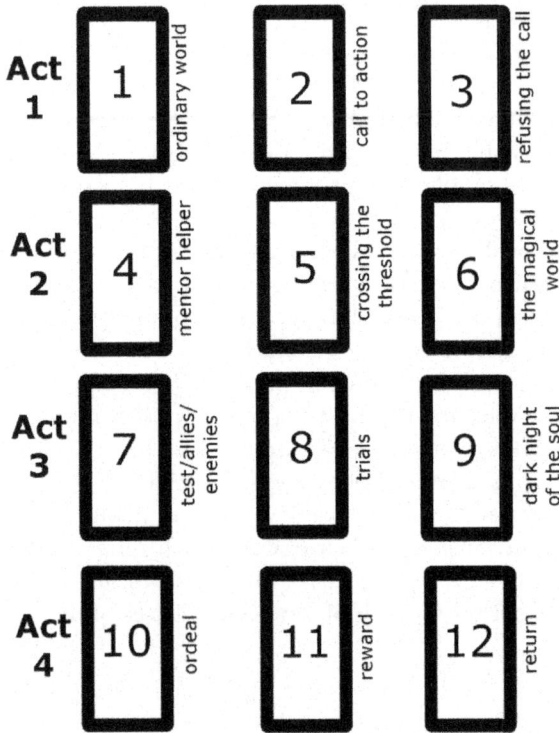

Act 1	1 — ordinary world	2 — call to action	3 — refusing the call
Act 2	4 — mentor helper	5 — crossing the threshold	6 — the magical world
Act 3	7 — test/allies/enemies	8 — trials	9 — dark night of the soul
Act 4	10 — ordeal	11 — reward	12 — return

From *Tarot for Fiction Writers* - www.thewritersaurus.com

The Hero's Journey Spread

This spread has been divided into four rows, each one representing one of the four acts (which is a three-act structure with the second act divided in half at the mid-point). Each card represents one of the twelve phases of the hero's journey.

Ordinary World: This is the set-up for what the world is like before the hero takes the journey. It may be what is at stake (the hero needs to take the journey to save the ordinary world) or it may be something the hero wants to escape from.

Example: In the 2003 Christmas film *Elf,* the lead character of Buddy is a human who was raised by elves at the North Pole. Even though the North Pole is a fantastical place to us, it's the ordinary world for Buddy.

Call to Action: Something happens that forces the hero to act.

Example: In *Elf,* Buddy learns that he's a human, and that his father is on the naughty list. Not only does Buddy need to go meet his father, but he has a goal: show his father the true meaning of Christmas.

Refusing the Call: This is where the hero has doubts or fears about undertaking the task. They may even think they are unworthy of it. This phase of the hero's journey seems to be one that is commonly omitted, especially in modern movies and literature.

Example: In *Harry Potter and the Sorcerer's Stone,* Harry tells Hagrid that he can't go to Hogwarts, that there's no way he's a wizard.

Mentor Helper: The mentor helper is an older, experienced person who helps the main character on their journey. They're usually introduced at this point in the story, though there's some leeway.

Example: In *Harry Potter and the Sorcerer's Stone,* Dumbledore is introduced after Harry crosses the threshold and is at Hogwarts. In *Elf,* Santa is the one who tells Buddy who his father is and that he must find him. In *The Hunger Games,* Katniss meets Haymitch, her coach, on the train ride to the Capitol.

Crossing the Threshold: This is the journey the hero undertakes to cross into the magical world.

Example: In *Harry Potter,* Harry rides the Hogwarts Express from London to Hogwarts, Buddy walks from the North Pole to New York City ("I passed through the seven levels of the Candy Cane forest, through the sea of swirly twirly gum drops, and then I walked through the Lincoln Tunnel"), and Katniss rides the train to the Capitol.

The Magical World: This is the new world that the character is introduced to.

Example: For Harry, it's the magical world of Hogwarts, for Buddy, it's New York City (resulting in a montage of holly-jolly hilarity), for Katniss, it's the Capitol.

Test/Allies/Enemies: Around this section of the story we learn where our character stands in the grand scheme of things, and who his friends and enemies are.

Example: In *Elf,* Buddy's new family and love interest are introduced, in *Harry Potter,* we learn about the four houses; meet Ron, Hermione, and Malfoy; and all the students are sorted into houses by the sorting hat. In *The Hunger Games,* we meet the other tributes and learn which ones are more trustworthy than others, and Katniss is subjected to a test and rating.

Tarot Tip:
Use the important relationships spread to find out more about your hero's friends and foes.

Trials: Trials make up the meat of the second act—these are all the obstacles the character must overcome leading up to achieving (or failing) their goal. You'll learn more about the second act in the Four-act Structure spread. If you're following a three-act structure, the trials take place in the first half of the second act, before the midpoint. Remember, trials consist of obstacles the hero must overcome.

Example: Buddy's trials in *Elf* are his job as an elf at Gimbles, working in the mail room, winning over his step-brother, Michael, and encountering the short-statured children's book author played by Peter Dinklage. It's notable that Buddy failed all but one of these trials (winning Michael's approval)—the hero should fail the majority, or if they succeed in one, that success should have unforeseen consequences or at least raise the stakes.

Dark Night of the Soul: The last trial should result in a spectacular failure, something that sends the hero into a downward spiral. Whatever plans they had are now ruined. They should literally give up at this point.

Example: In *Elf*, Buddy's candidness with Peter Dinklage's character causes his father to throw him out. Buddy leaves, writing a note that says, "I don't belong anywhere." He goes to a bridge, which strongly suggests he is about to commit suicide (pretty dark for a Christmas flick).

Ordeal: This is the big battle. If the story has an antagonist, they and the hero face off. It is likely that the hero will have to go into a version of a "dark world." This confrontation will change the hero forever. They may even physically die and come back to life.

Example: In *The Hunger Games,* the dark world is the arena; in *Harry Potter and the Sorcerer's Stone* it's past Fluffy in the forbidden corridor.

Reward: This is what the hero receives for their victory.

Example: In *The Hunger Games,* Katniss and Peeta both get to live, and they are celebrated across Panem. In *Elf,* Buddy finds the family that he's always wanted, and finally feels like he belongs.

Return: The hero returns to their ordinary world, but they and their circumstances are forever changed.

Example: In *Harry Potter,* Harry goes back to the Dursley's—but he now knows the truth about his heritage, and can even use it to keep his cousin, aunt, and uncle from picking on him. In *The Hunger Games,* Katniss and Peeta return to District 12, but they must live with the wrath of President Snow hanging over their heads. The last scene in *Elf* is Buddy visiting his adoptive father at the North Pole—along with his wife and new daughter.

Questions:
Are all of these events necessary in my story?
Are any of these events combined into one scene?

Tarot Tip:
The hero's journey may seem like a plot structure (and it is), but it is closely tied with your character's arc. By the end, the character should have changed in some fundamental way.

Consider the first card and the last card, and then look at each of the cards between them and map where that character is in their arc. How will you show that in your writing?

Variation:

There are many different variations of the hero's journey floating around the Internet. Feel free to change the steps above to suit your own needs. Don't feel like you need to adhere to this structure too closely—the cards should support the story, not the other way around. And remember, you may occasionally feel like a card (or cards) are irrelevant to the questions you're asking. It's okay to ignore them—but do take the time to fully consider them before you do so.

Four-Act Story Structure

The most common story structure you'll see is three-act structure. The popularity of this structure has never made much sense to me. Sure, the first act is easy enough. It contains the set-up and the inciting incident. The third act isn't too bad, either—it contains the climax and ending.

But that leaves the majority of the book to the second act, which generally contains no guideposts at all. Consequently, the second act can end up with pacing that is either too fast or too slow.

Many writers remedy this by adding the "midpoint" smack dab in the middle of the second act, dividing it in two. So why not just call the midpoint what it is—the break between the second and the third act, with a fourth act to follow?

Here's the breakdown of four-act structure. You'll notice that **acts one and three are virtually the same as in traditional three-act structure**; the only difference is that we break the gigantic second act into two more easily-managed chunks.

Act One: Act one is where everything is set up. We're introduced to the protagonist and the ordinary world. The factors of the story problem are put into place. The inciting incident happens towards the end.

Act Two: The protagonist crosses the threshold into the "magical world" (see the previous section about the hero's journey). They meet new friends, and first learn about the final trial they are going to face. The majority of this act is taken up by trials—the number of which depends on your genre and how long the book is. All of these trials should be failed, or succeeded in such a way that it makes things worse (see Yes, But.../No, And... Spread on page 66 for more info). The last trial is failed so badly that all hope seems completely lost, and the character enters the dark night of the soul.

Act Three: The third act begins with the book's mid-point. Something happens that makes the character decide to try one more time. Possible catalysts for this decision include learning a key bit of information, a pep talk from another character, or a crazy idea coming to them. The rest of the act is taken up by the character gathering resources and allies and forming the plan. It ends with the lead-up to the final battle, or entering the "dark world."

Act Four: The final battle takes place. The hero either wins or loses. The battle is followed by the wind-down, tying up loose ends, and showing the new status quo.

Questions:
What is the defining tone of each act?
Does the tone stay consistent throughout, or does it change dramatically?

Four-Act Spread

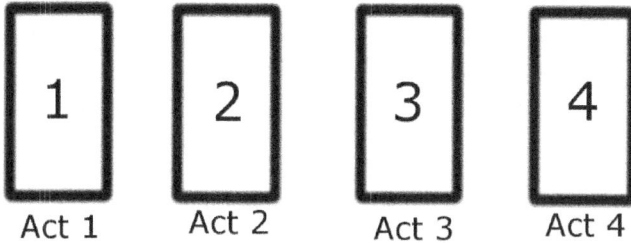

From *Tarot for Fiction Writers - www.thewritersaurus.com*

The Four-Act Spread

Shuffle the deck and lay out four cards in a line. Card 1 refers to Act One, card 2 refers to Act Two, and so on.

Variation 1:

Shuffle and lay out the cards as indicated above, but instead of letting each card represent an entire act, use the cards to represent the plot points within each act. So card 1 represents the status quo of the ordinary world, card 2 represents the inciting incident, card 3 represents the midpoint, and card 4 represents the climax—we'll go into these points more in The Rising Action Spread on page 63.

Tarot Tip:

Do this spread for each of your different books, then your series as a whole!

Example Spread (From My Own Tarot Journal)

I decided to do this spread for the first book in my *Pagewalker* series. I had a general idea of how I wanted the plot to go, but it was still very amorphous.

Card 1: Reversed Eight of Swords
Card 2: Three of Swords
Card 3: Reversed Nine of Wands
Card 4: Reversed Page of Cups

Example Analysis

This spread was one that really didn't go as I expected it to, but the insight I got from it was intense. This is a prime example of how tarot can put you into a creative state. I wrote stream of conscious notes on the plot of this book for a good forty minutes after I did this spread.

The first thing I noticed was that the spread was very negative on the whole. Three of the four cards were reversed, and the one that wasn't was the Three of Swords, the heartache card.

Nothing in the cards immediately jumped out at me, so I mentally went through the plot points and scenes to try to place them in the four-act structure. I didn't concentrate too much on the meanings of the cards.

Once I'd done that, I went through each card and related it to its corresponding act:

Act One/Reversed Eight of Swords: Self-sacrifice, respite, new beginnings. Mae's time as the Pagewalker is over, and April's is just beginning. It was also while considering the meaning of this card that I realized I needed to get into the action faster than I'd originally planned. I'd planned to have April work at the library for a few days before she discovered Dorian and the portal, but I need to get that hook in as close to the beginning as possible.

Act Two/Three of Swords: Heartache. After seeing this card, I realized that April and Dorian are going through similar experiences. Dorian lost Mae, the most important matriarchal figure in his life, and April is dealing with losing her grandmother in the near future. Perhaps Dorian can talk to her about this?

Act Three/Reversed Nine of Wands: Jealousy, dispute. Thaddeus and April talk at (not to!) each other over the future of the library. It is a battle of the wits, rather than a physical or magical fight, as Thaddeus insisted that they go without magic because he wouldn't need it.

Act Four/Reversed Page of Cups: Unpleasant surprises. Andre is killed after opening a Heart of Darkness while checking the library after April goes home.

Rising Action

This spread is based on the classic plot diagram. Remember that? If you don't, you probably skipped a lot of high school English class.

The basic purpose of a plot diagram is to create a visual representation of the stakes and/or tension in a story. Here is a simple example:

Simple Plot Diagram

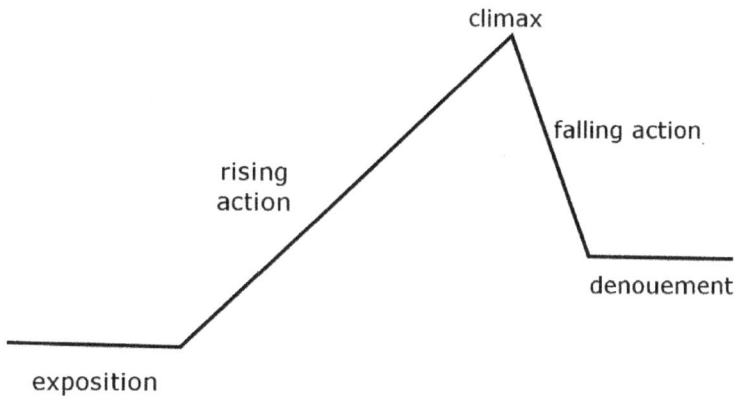

climax

falling action

rising
action

denouement

exposition

From *Tarot for Fiction Writers - www.thewritersaurus.com*

Exposition: This is where the status quo is established and the characters and story problem are introduced. The inciting incident takes place at the end of the exposition. This is when the story's tension first begins to ratchet up.

Example: In *The Hunger Games,* we're introduced to Katniss Everdeen and shown everyday life in District 12. The inciting incident is Katniss volunteering to take Prim's place.

Rising Action: Hero and friends face a series of obstacles. With each obstacle, the stakes are raised and the things the hero must do are more harrowing. There should be at least two obstacles. The rising action also includes the midpoint, which catapults the character into the second half of the story and towards the climax.

Example: Katniss faces several obstacles, including training, the test where she will be graded, and the talk show where she must convince the world that she is worth loving. The midpoint comes when she enters the arena.

The Climax: The climax is the high point of the story. The final battle takes place and the hero faces off with the antagonist, if there is one.

Example: Katniss and Peeta decide to commit suicide together rather than play by the Gamemakers' rules, forcing them to let both of them live.

Falling Action: The hero has either won or lost. Everything starts to move towards the new status quo.

Example: Katniss and Peeta tour Panem before returning to District 12.

Denouement: Everything has settled and the new status quo is established. If this is a series, the seeds of the next installment's problem are planted.

Example: Katniss and Peeta return to the victor's quarters in District 12, knowing they are under the watchful gaze of President Snow. They will have to keep up their act for the rest of their lives.

Just like the hero's journey, there are infinite versions of plot diagrams. Some map the rising and falling tension so that they end up looking like a cardiograph. The basis for this spread is the simple one above. The line is flat as we establish the status quo, then starts to spike after the inciting incident. After the inciting incident comes the obstacles (at least two of them, though you can add more) and the midpoint, then everything spikes at the climax, after which things ratchet down, quickly returning to a new baseline, the "new" status quo.

Rising Action Spread

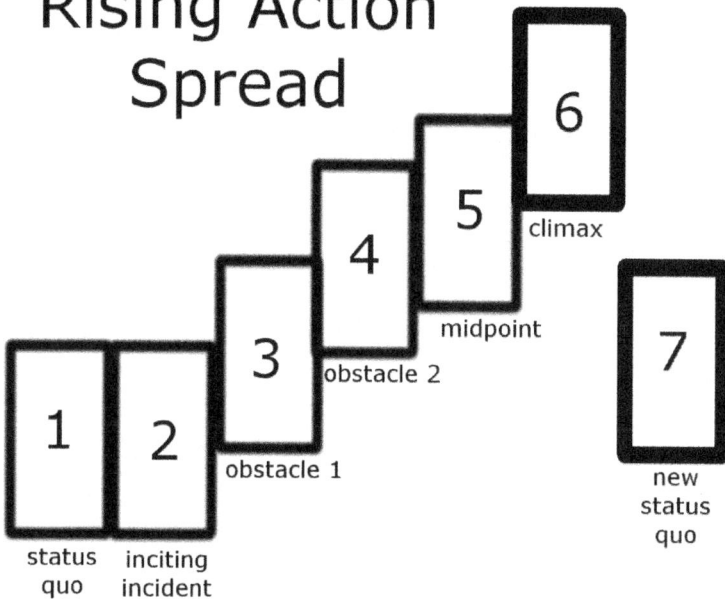

From *Tarot for Fiction Writers* - www.thewritersaurus.com

The Rising Action Spread

Shuffle and cut your deck, then lay out seven cards in the shape you see above. Card 1 represents the normal world at the beginning; it is either what the hero must fight to protect, what they will lose, or what they want to escape from. Card 2 represents the inciting incident, the incident that throws the plot in motion. Cards 3 and 4 represent the first two obstacles that the hero must face. Card 5 represents the midpoint, the point where everything changes—for the worse. Card 6 is the climax, or final battle. The last card represents the new status quo.

Questions:

Do these cards refer to events, ideas, or people?
Does my plot need more obstacle cards?

Yes, but... / No, and...

At first glance, "Yes, but..." and "no, and..." may seem like near nonsense, but they are two of the most important phrases in fiction writing.

They are the answers to the question, "Did the protagonists' plan work?" At least, these are the only answers if you want to write engaging fiction. The basic concept behind them is that no matter what your characters do, their situation just keeps getting worse. The only time the answer is, "Yes, the plan worked" with no qualifiers is at the end of your story.

Examples:

Did Katniss' plan to save her and Peeta from having to kill one another in the arena work? **Yes, BUT** now she's on President Snow's radar.

In the season two finale of *Buffy the Vampire Slayer,* did Willow succeed in turning Angelus back into Angel in time to save him? **No, AND** she turned him back into Angel a moment too late, so that Buffy was forced to sentence the man she loved to an eternity of torment.

This works especially well for serials and series, because what gets you out of an immediate life-or-death situation will have repercussions in future installments, as can be seen in the above example from *The Hunger Games.*

Yes, But.../No, And...
Spread

yes/no   but/and

From Tarot for Fiction Writers - www.thewritersaurus.com

Yes, but... / No, and... spread

Draw two cards and lay them out side-by-side as in the above graphic. Card 1 represents your character's method for solving a problem, and card 2 represents the complications that arise from it. If card 1 is reversed, then their plan failed. If it is upright, it succeeded. Card 2 is either the "BUT" or the "AND."

Questions:

Are these complications (what's making the situation worse) derived directly from the character's actions? If not, consider revising.
Do I have enough try/fail cycles? Do I have too many?

Tarot Tip:

This spread is also helpful for dealing with writer's block or to further develop a story prompt, because it helps you add complications and ratchet up the stakes.

Spreads for World Building

World Builder's Disease

One thing you have to watch out for when world building is that you don't do *too* much of it. Many writers spend months or even years "perfecting" their story world. It's up to you just how much world building your work needs, but if you repeatedly put off writing in order to develop your story world, you most likely have "world builder's disease."

But isn't a well-developed world a *good* thing? Of course. However, there's a point where it turns from a positive into a hindrance. The reason is two-fold. One, you're not writing. Two, when (and if) you start writing, you'll be tempted to include all that world-building in the text, which will make your story boring to ninety-nine percent of readers.

There are two things that cause world builder's disease. The first is lack of confidence. The writer doubts their abilities and senses that their writing won't live up to their own expectations, so they just keep developing their world, characters, and plot. They can keep up the illusion of writing without having to face the possibility that it won't be as good as it is in their head. The second thing that causes world builder's disease is the fact that writing is hard and world building is easy. The cure in either case is to start writing.

Of course, each genre has its own standards and expectations. Writers of science fiction and fantasy will spend more time world building than writers of contemporary romance or YA. You also need to consider what you want to get out of your writing. Is your goal to make money and/or be as widely read as possible? Then you'll want to spend the minimum amount of time world building as possible.

But if you're of that rarer breed of writer who writes for the pleasure of it, then feel free to world build to your heart's content. Or perhaps your target audience expects page-long explanations of each character's lineage. That's fine. Just know that most readers won't.

Know yourself and know your readers.

Diagnosing World Builder's Disease Spread

writing goal

From *Tarot for Fiction Writers* - *www.thewritersaurus.com*

A Spread for Diagnosing the Cause of Your World Builder's Disease

Unlike the other spreads in this book, which deal with your story, this spread is about *you*. It's designed to help you figure out what is causing your world builder's disease. To use it, shuffle and cut your deck, then lay out two cards in the positions shown in the above diagram. Card 1 will help you determine what your writing goals are. Fame? Fortune? Validation? Something else? Card 2 represents the conflict or fear that is keeping you from achieving that goal.

Questions:

Am I writing this book for myself or for others?
Am I doing anything to sabotage myself?
Are my actions really helping me to fulfill my goals?
What am I afraid of?

World Building: Only the Essentials

If our goal is to prevent world builder's disease, how do we know how much world building we need?

There are two questions that can help you answer that:

1. **What are the differences between the story world and our world?** This is important, because readers will assume the story world is like ours in any given way unless told differently.

2. **Does this difference relate to the story?** Answering this question is essential for both preventing world builder's disease and for making sure you do not spend too much time and effort developing aspects of your story that won't make it into your book.

Think about it: If you spend days and days writing up the anatomy and history about a fictional species of dragon that only ever appears flying above your characters' heads, isn't that time wasted?

However, if your protagonist is a dragon expert, then that information may be necessary to have. It all depends on your story.

If you're like me, you'll probably get sudden flashes of insight into aspects of the world that don't fit into your current plot. That's fine. Write them down, but don't spend any effort or time actively developing them. If you're writing a series, you'll probably find these aspects become relevant later on. You can develop them at that point.

Essential World Building Questions Spread

1	**2**
difference from our world	relation to plot

From *Tarot for Fiction Writers* - www.thewritersaurus.com

The Essential World Building Questions Spread

This spread is good for genres of speculative fiction, such as fantasy, science fiction, and dystopian fiction. Use it to determine what aspects of your world building are necessary and which are not.

Shuffle and cut the deck, then lay out two cards in the above formation. Card 1 shows an essential difference between the story world and our "regular" world. Card two tells us if and how this difference relates to the plot.

Questions:

If the difference does not relate to the current plot, could it possibly affect things in the future?

Is the world completely separate from our own (like Game of Thrones *or* The Lord of the Rings), *or is it contained within ours (like* The Hunger Games *or* The Dresden Files)?

Spreads for Writer's Block

The One-Card Wonder Spread—It's Back!

Just when you thought it was safe to dive back in the pages of Tarot for Fiction Writers...

No matter how well I plan my stories, I always get to those points where I'm staring at a blank screen, not sure what to write next.

Does this mean I need to spend more time planning? I don't think so. There's a point where you have to start writing. Sometimes you need to start writing to know what you need to know to write (say that three times fast!).

That doesn't mean I like it, though. I usually write thousands of words a day, but a moment like this can drop my productivity down to mere sentences, no matter how much I try to write through the block. Until I started to use the tarot, I just accepted this as part of the process. Some days were good writing days and some days weren't.

But shortly after starting to write this book, I thought, *I wonder if I can use the tarot as a tool for beating writer's block?* I've always believed that true writer's block was caused by creative fatigue, and/or the inability to look at a story problem from a different angle. Since we use tarot to replenish our creative soil and see things from a different perspective, it's reasonable to think that the tarot might be just the tool for conquering writer's block.

One-Card
Wonder Spread

```
┌───────┐
│       │
│   1   │
│       │
└───────┘
```

From *Tarot for Fiction Writers - www.thewritersaurus.com*

The One-Card Wonder Spread

I wanted this spread to be super-simple. We're not starting a new tarot brainstorming session, after all. We're simply trying to get past a block.

For this spread, it's important to move away from wherever you've been writing. Since that's where you've been while experiencing the block, staying there will only reinforce it. Spend some time doing something else—listening to music, reading a book, or meditating. Set a timer. Twenty minutes, maybe. When the timer goes off, take out your cards and shuffle them. Then pull out a single card. This card is the answer to your problems. You may need to consider the card for several minutes. Repeat as needed.

Questions:

Do any of the card's symbols correspond to your story problem?
Does the card tell you the reason for your block? What can you do to fix it?

Creating Your Own Spreads

The next step for you is to create your own spreads. The wonderful thing about doing this is that you can tailor them to your needs so that you get the maximum benefit from them. You can do pretty much anything; much like the fiction you write, the form and function of the spreads you create are limited only by your imagination.

You may have already started modifying the spreads in this book. That's good. In fact, several of the spreads in this book were inspired by commonly used tarot spreads. The conflict cross was loosely based off of the Celtic cross, for example. There are countless resources where you can find inspiration, including books, blogs, and groups on Facebook. I have listed several in the resources section at the end of the book.

Below are the steps for creating your own tarot spread:

1. **Decide what you want your spread to do.** Why are you creating the spread? What do you want to get out of it? Do you want a spread that will help you plot your story, or a spread that will help with character development?

2. **Choose a shape.** You can pretty much do whatever you want, shape-wise. The main concern is that you want it to be easy to read. I also like the shape to be symbolic, because it can help you remember what each position means.

3. **Keep it simple.** Resist the urge to make things too complicated, especially at first. There are spreads that use the entire deck, but that may be overwhelming. Limit your first spread to four cards or less.

4. **Take notes.**
   Note down any spreads you create in your journal. That way you can refer to it in the future, and make any changes.

Exercise 8: Go ahead and create your first spread following the steps above. If you'd like, you can begin by modifying one of the spreads in this book. Be sure to send a picture of your original spreads to hdukeauthor@gmail.com! I'd love to see them!

A Few Last Words

I wracked my brain trying to figure out how to end this, to find the perfect pearls of wisdom to dispense and the right truth bombs to drop. But then I realized you're like me: you have a lot of things to do and not enough time to do them.

So I'll just say thanks for reading. I hope you've found this book useful, and that it added a few tricks to your writing arsenal. If it did, please consider leaving an honest review on Amazon. It helps other writers who will benefit from reading this book find it and helps me decide whether to write more books like it.

If you want more guidance on using the tarot in your writing, check out *The Fiction Writer's Tarot Journal,* a guided workbook designed to help you find success in your own tarot journey. If you're not sure where to start with your own journal, it's a great option. You can buy it on Amazon, or download a printable version when you sign up for updates from The Writersaurus. Visit www.thewritersaurus.com/freetarotjournal to sign up.

Want to stay in touch? Join The Writersaurus Facebook Group! It's the easiest place to stay in touch with me directly, not to mention that there are some amazing, talented, helpful people in that group. I look forward to talking to you there!

LET'S STAY IN TOUCH!
YOU'RE INVITED TO ...

THE WRITERSAURUS FACEBOOK GROUP

ALL CREATIVES WELCOME
FACEBOOK.COM/GROUPS/THEWRITERSAURUS

Want more writerly advice? There are four years' worth of free articles and resources over on thewritersaurus.com.

Now what are you waiting for? **Go write!**

—*Haley Dziuk, AKA The Writersaurus*

Exercise 9: This is the last exercise, and it may be the most important one in the book. Take a few minutes to plan at least one way you will actively use the information you've learned in this book to better your writing. The majority of readers who read this book (and any other writing book) will not actually use the lessons they've learned. Don't be one of those people. If you haven't done the exercises, completing them is a good place to start.

Glossary

Court Cards (character cards): These are the sixteen "royalty" or "face" cards in the Minor Arcana. Each suit has four court cards: the king, the queen, the knight, and the page. The king, queen, and knight correspond to the king, queen, and jack in a deck of playing cards. A list of the court cards and their meanings can be found on page 122.

Major Arcana: These are the twenty-two "archetype" cards. This suit includes some of the most famous cards of the tarot: the fool, death, and the devil. There is no equivalent in a regular fifty-two-card deck. The Major Arcana card meanings can be found on page 98.

Minor Arcana: The Minor Arcana are the fifty-six situation and character cards. The Minor Arcana is divided into four suits: Wands, Cups, Swords, and Pentacles. Each suit has fourteen cards. Cards 1-10 are numbered, and cards 10-14 are the face cards (Page, Knight, Queen, King).

Numbered cards: These are cards 1-10 in each suit of the Minor Arcana. These cards refer to everyday situations. The meanings of the numbered Minor Arcana cards are listed on page 139.

Position: This refers to where a card is placed in a tarot spread.

Reversed: When a card is laid out upside down, it is reversed. Reversed cards have different meanings than upright cards—usually it is an opposite or extreme version of the upright meaning.

Spread: A spread is the layout or shape the cards are laid out in for a reading.

Suit: The Minor Arcana is divided into four suits: Wands, Cups, Swords, and Pentacles, which correspond to the four suits of a regular deck of playing cards (Wands = Clubs, Cups = Hearts, Swords = Spades, Pentacles = Diamonds). There are fourteen cards in each suit of the tarot (the suits of a regular deck of playing cards only have thirteen cards each, because there is no corresponding Page card).

Trump Card: This is another term for a Major Arcana card.

Upright: An upright card is a card that is not upside down, or reversed.

Exercises

Exercise 1: Choose a tarot deck. Spend some time looking at sample art and reading reviews. Do you like the images and symbols, and do they spark your creativity? Alternatively, head to your local book shop or New Age store. Once you have them, flip through them and familiarize yourself with the imagery. Don't worry about the meanings yet.

Exercise 2: Choose your first tarot journal, and label it as such. Don't forget a writing utensil!

Exercise 3: Separate out the Major Arcana from your deck. Using the descriptions above (or the ones listed in the booklet that came with your deck), go through the cards one by one and try to relate their descriptions or imagery to your story in some way. If you are not currently working on a story, try to relate them to books, television shows, or movies. The purpose of this is to get you to start seeing the cards through a narrative lens.

Exercise 4: This is the most beneficial exercise in this book! During the course of your tarot journey you'll want to write down the meaning of each card in your tarot journal **by hand**. I suggest starting by going through the cards in your deck one by one, and pulling out two or three cards that appeal to you. Before looking up their meanings, consider each card and write down your impressions of it (writing out a description of the card's illustration REALLY helps you remember its meaning!). Then refer to either the section on card meanings on page 98 or the pamphlet that came with your deck.
Repeat this process over the course of a few weeks until you've written meanings for each card. As you get acquainted with and use the cards, your understanding of their meanings will deepen. Continue to write these insights down in your journal.
Be sure to order the entries in such a way that you can easily find them later.

Exercise 5: Follow the directions for the One-Card Question Spread on page 20. Be sure to record your results in your journal.

Exercise 6: Create a list of at least four other questions you could ask the one card question spread about your story.

Exercise 7: Take out your notes and write down your antagonist's motivation. If he doesn't have one, lay out the conflict cross spread for them. Try to see their situation from their eyes. In their own head, they should be the hero.

Exercise 8: Go ahead and create your first spread following the steps listed on page 74. If you'd like, you can begin by modifying one of the spreads in this book. Be sure to send a picture of your original spreads to hdukeauthor@gmail.com! I'd love to see them!

Exercise 9: This is the last exercise, and it may be the most important one in the book. Take a few minutes to plan at least one way you will actively use the information you've learned in this book to better your writing. The majority of readers who read this book (and any other writing book) will not actually use the lessons they've learned. Don't be one of those people. If you haven't done the exercises, start there.

The Spreads

One-Card Question Spread

```
┌─────┐
│     │
│  1  │
│     │
└─────┘
```

Answer

From *Tarot for Fiction Writers* - www.thewritersaurus.com

Spread One: The One-Card Question Spread
Directions: This simple spread is used to answer a single question. The example question is *what is my story about?,* but you can use any question you wish. Go to page 20 for more in-depth instructions.

One-Card Story Prompt Spread

```
┌─────────┐
│         │
│    1    │
│         │
└─────────┘
```
Prompt

From *Tarot for Fiction Writers* - www.thewritersaurus.com

Spread Two: The One-Card Story Prompt Spread

Directions: This is another simple one. Shuffle and cut the deck, then draw a single card. This card is a prompt for a new story. Set a timer and write for fifteen minutes. This is a great daily exercise, especially if you're not working on a larger project. Go to page 24 for more in-depth directions.

Goal, Motivation, and Conflict Spread

  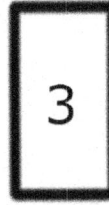

Goal   Motivation   Conflict

From *Tarot for Fiction Writers* - www.thewritersaurus.com

Spread Three: The Goal, Motivation, and Conflict Spread
Directions: Shuffle and cut the deck, and lay out three cards in the above formation. Flip to page 26 for more in-depth directions.
Card 1: The character's goal (the thing they want to achieve)
Card 2: The character's motivation (the reason they want to achieve the goal)
Card 3: The conflict (the thing preventing them from achieving their goal)

Character Cross Spread

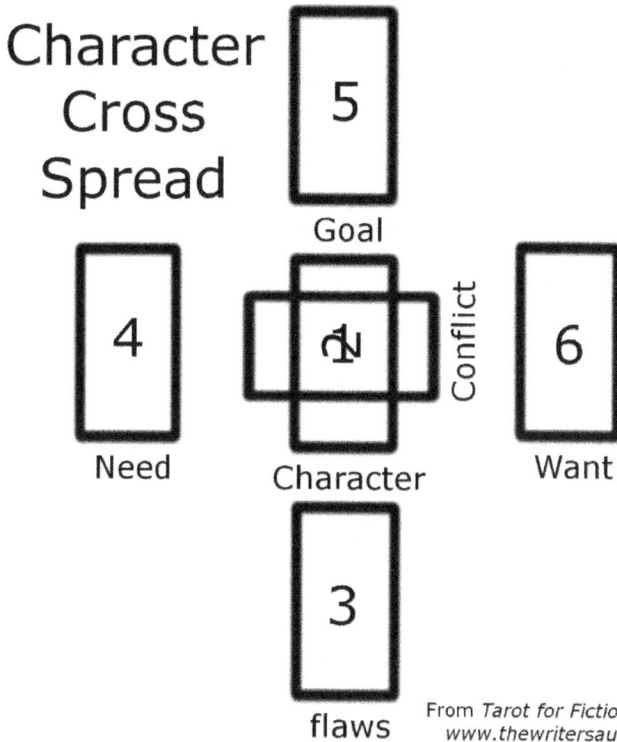

Goal

Need   Character   Want

Conflict

flaws

From *Tarot for Fiction Writers*
www.thewritersaurus.com

Spread Four: The Conflict Cross Spread

Directions: shuffle and cut the deck, then lay out six cards in the above formation. Go to page 31 for more in-depth instructions.

Card 1: The character

Card 2: The conflict (the thing preventing the character from achieving their goal)

Card 3: The character's flaws and weaknesses (these cause or compound the conflict)

Card 4: The character's need (why they need to achieve the goal)

Card 5: The character's goal (what they want to achieve)

Card 6: The character's want (why they want to achieve the goal)

Backstory Spread

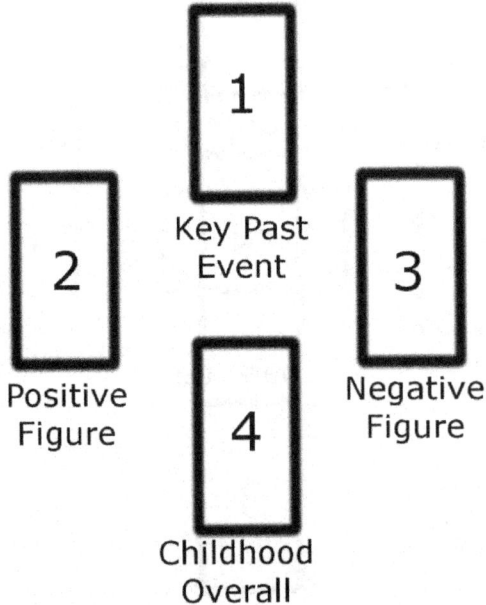

1

Key Past
Event

2

Positive
Figure

3

Negative
Figure

4

Childhood
Overall

From *Tarot for Fiction Writers* - www.thewritersaurus.com

Spread Five: The Backstory Spread

Directions: Shuffle and cut the deck, then lay out four cards in the above formation. Flip to page 34 for more in-depth instructions.

Card 1: Key event in the character's past (this event somehow causes, informs, or compounds the current crisis)

Card 2: Positive figure (a mentor or family member that had a positive influence on them)

Card 3: Negative figure (someone who had a negative impact on them, perhaps they caused the current story problem)

Card 4: Childhood/past overall (how their childhood or past was overall. Was it negative or positive?)

```
       Key
   Relationships        3
     Spread
                        C

   MC = main character
      C = character     6
      R = relationship
                        R

    4      7      1      5      2

    C      R     MC      R      C
```

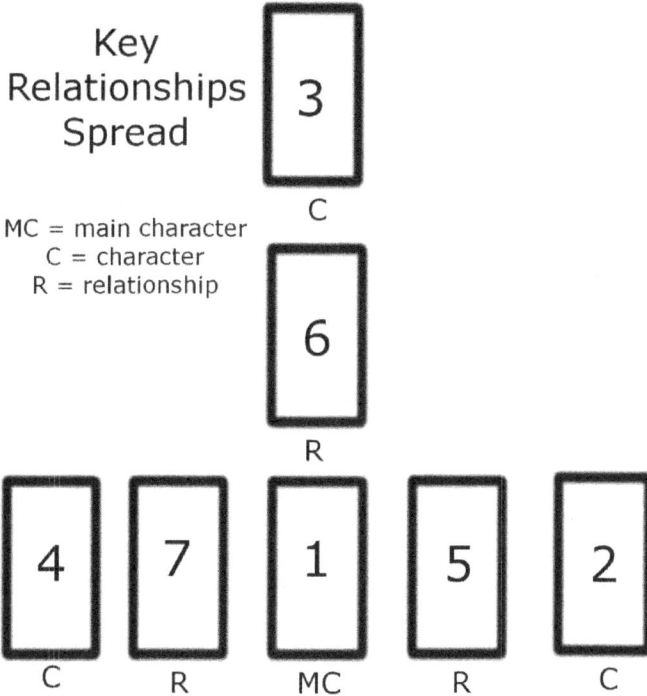

From Tarot for Fiction Writers - www.thewritersaurus.com

Spread Six: The Key Relationships Spread

Directions: shuffle and cut the deck, then lay out seven cards in the above formation. Go to page 38 for more in-depth instructions.

Card 1: the main character
Card 2: character two
Card 3: character three
Card 4: character four
Card 5: relationship between the main character and character two
Card 6: relationship between the main character and character three
Card 7: relationship between the main character and character four

One-on-One
Relationship Spread

C1 = character 1
C2 = character 2
R = relationship

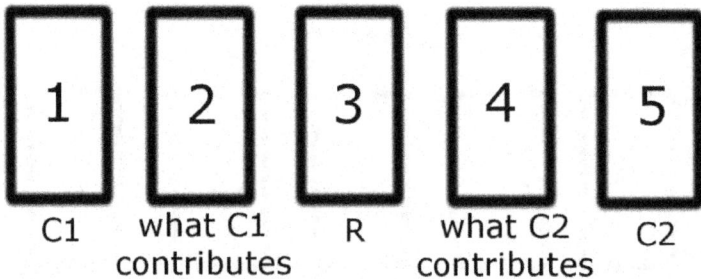

C1 | what C1 contributes | R | what C2 contributes | C2

From *Tarot for Fiction Writers* - *www.thewritersaurus.com*

Spread Seven: The One-on-One Relationship Spread

Directions: Shuffle and cut the deck, then lay out five cards in the above formation. This spread is designed to develop the relationship between two characters. For more in-depth instruction, turn to page 41.

Card 1: character one
Card 2: what character one contributes to the relationship
Card 3: the relationship overall
Card 4: what character two contributes to the relationship
Card 5: character two

Five-Man Band Spread

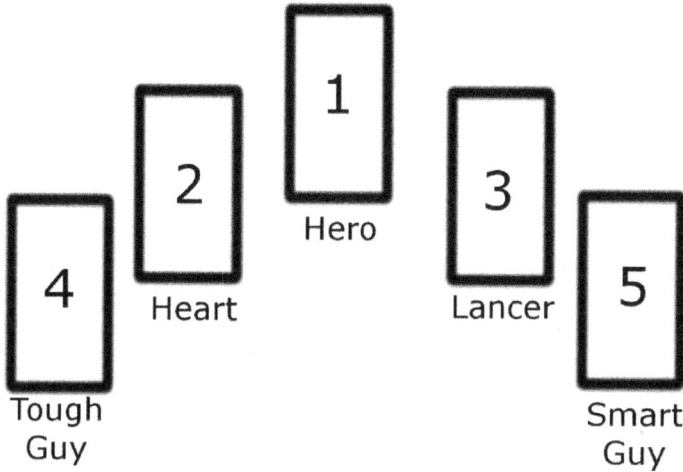

From *Tarot for Fiction Writers* - www.thewritersaurus.com

Spread Eight: The Five-Man Band Spread

Directions: shuffle and cut the deck, then lay out five cards in the above formation. First lay out and read the character cards, then lay out and read the secondary role cards. For more in-depth instructions, go to page 44.

Card 1: The Hero
Card 2: The Heart
Card 3: The Lancer
Card 4: The Tough Guy
Card 5: The Smart Guy

Five-Man Band Spread

(Variation)

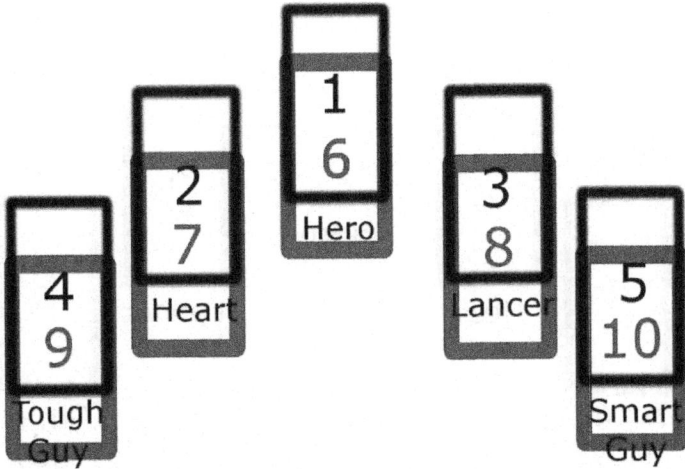

From *Tarot for Fiction Writers* - www.thewritersaurus.com

Spread Eight-and-a-Half: A Variation on the Five-Man Band Spread

Directions: Lay out cards 1-5 as directed for the Five-Man Band Spread. After you have completed the reading for these cards, lay out five more, one on top of each character card, as shown in blue above. These cards represent the secondary interests for each character. Turn to page 45 for more in-depth instructions.

Power Trio Spread

1

ethos character
(hero)

2

logos
character

3

pathos
character

From *Tarot for Fiction Writers* - www.thewritersaurus.com

Spread Nine: The Power Trio Spread
Directions: shuffle and cut the deck, then lay out seven cards in the above formation. Flip to page 50 for more in-depth instructions.
Card 1: Ethos (the Hero)
Card 2: Logos (the smart, logical friend)
Card 3: Pathos (the vulnerable, emotional friend)

Power Trio Spread
(variation)

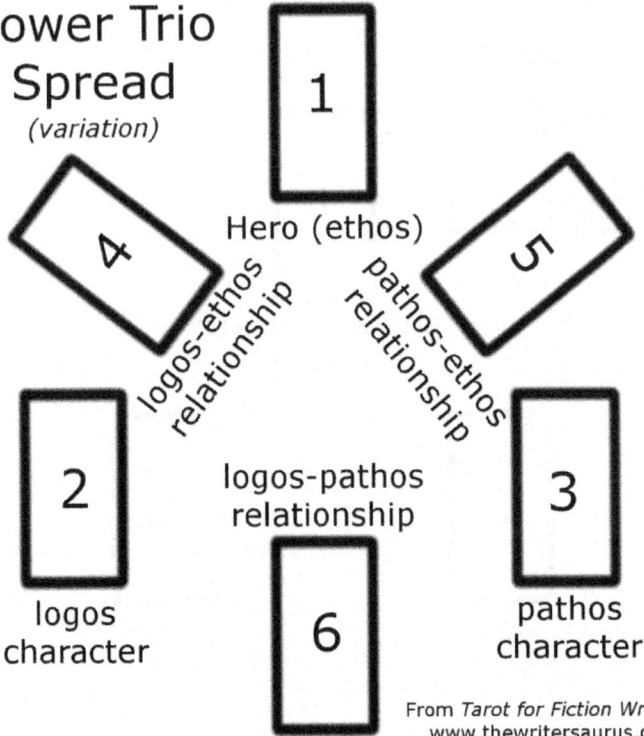

1

Hero (ethos)

4

5

logos-ethos relationship

pathos-ethos relationship

2

logos-pathos relationship

3

logos character

6

pathos character

From *Tarot for Fiction Writers* -
www.thewritersaurus.com

Spread Nine-and-a-Half: A Variation on the Power Trio Spread
Directions: Lay out The Power Trio Spread as directed, then lay out cards 4-6 as shown above. These represent the relationships between each of the members of the power trio. For more in-depth instructions, go to page 51.
Card 4: relationship between the hero and the logical friend
Card 5: relationship between the hero and the emotional friend
Card 6: relationship between the logical friend and emotional friend

Hero's Journey Spread

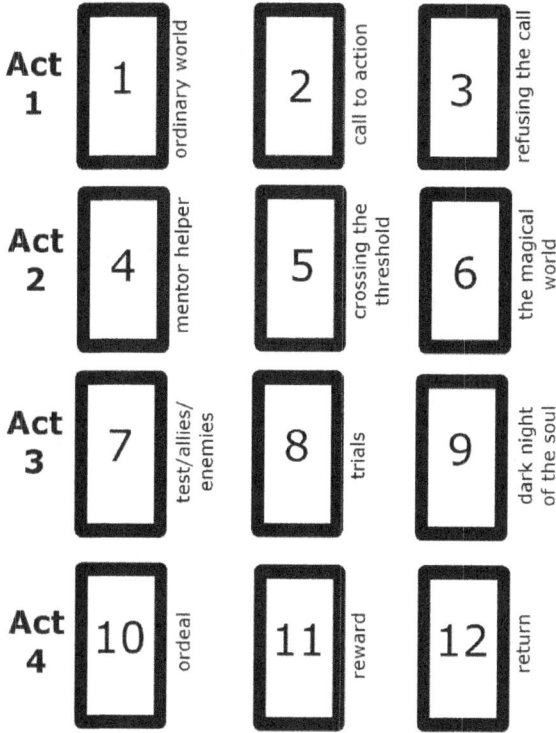

Act 1	1 — ordinary world	2 — call to action	3 — refusing the call
Act 2	4 — mentor helper	5 — crossing the threshold	6 — the magical world
Act 3	7 — test/allies/enemies	8 — trials	9 — dark night of the soul
Act 4	10 — ordeal	11 — reward	12 — return

From *Tarot for Fiction Writers* - www.thewritersaurus.com

Spread Ten: The Hero's Journey Spread

Directions: shuffle and cut the deck, then lay out the cards in the above formation. For more in-depth instructions, go to page 56.

Card 1: the ordinary world
Card 2: call to action
Card 3: refusing the call
Card 4: the mentor helper
Card 5: crossing the threshold
Card 6: the magical world
Card 7: test/allies/enemies
Card 8: trials
Card 9: dark night of the soul (black moment)
Card 10: ordeal
Card 11: reward
Card 12: return

Four-Act Spread

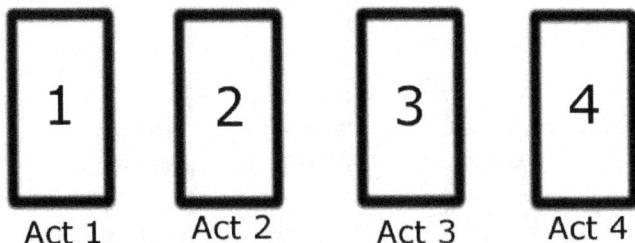

| 1 | 2 | 3 | 4 |

Act 1   Act 2   Act 3   Act 4

From *Tarot for Fiction Writers - www.thewritersaurus.com*

Spread Eleven: Four-Act Story Spread

Directions: Shuffle and cut the deck, then lay four cards out in the above formation. Turn to page 61 for more in-depth instructions.

Card 1: Act One
Card 2: Act Two
Card 3: Act Three
Card 4: Act Four

Rising Action Spread

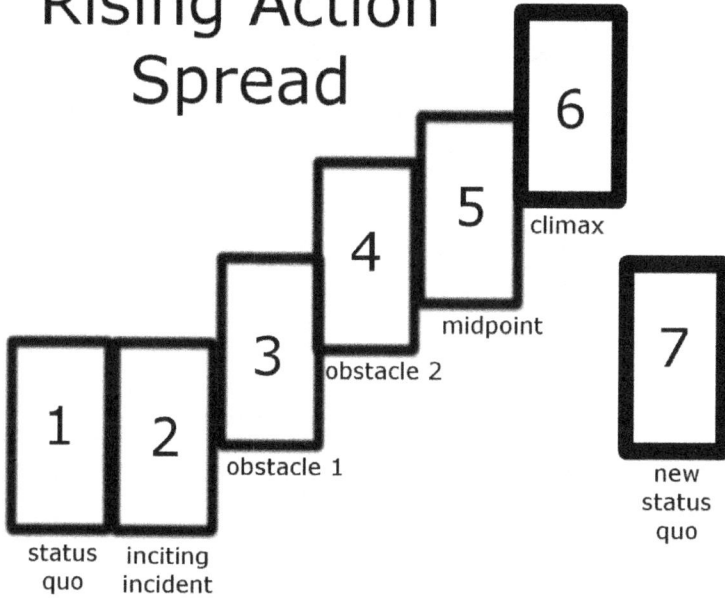

Card positions:
- **1** — status quo
- **2** — inciting incident
- **3** — obstacle 1
- **4** — obstacle 2
- **5** — midpoint
- **6** — climax
- **7** — new status quo

From *Tarot for Fiction Writers - www.thewritersaurus.com*

Spread Twelve: The Rising Action Spread

Directions: Shuffle and cut the deck, then lay out seven cards in the above formation. Flip to page 65 for more in-depth instructions.

Card 1: the status quo
Card 2: the inciting incident
Card 3: obstacle one
Card 4: obstacle two
Card 5: midpoint
Card 6: climax
Card 7: the new status quo

Yes, But.../No, And... Spread

yes/no

but/and

From Tarot for Fiction Writers - www.thewritersaurus.com

Spread Thirteen: Yes, But.../No, And... Spread

Directions: shuffle and cut the deck, then lay out two cards in the above formation. This spread can be used to decide whether or not a character's plan works (hint: whether it works or not, things get worse!) Go to page 66 for more in-depth instructions.

Card 1: if the card is upright, then their plan worked, but it made things worse. If it is reversed, their plan didn't work, and it made things worse.

Card 2: Card two describes how things get worse.

Diagnosing World Builder's Disease Spread

From *Tarot for Fiction Writers - www.thewritersaurus.com*

Spread Fourteen: A Spread to Diagnose the Cause of Your World Builder's Disease

This spread is used to diagnose and treat the causes of world builder's disease. For more information on world builder's disease, go to the section on world building.

Directions: shuffle and cut the deck, then lay out two cards in the above positions. Turn to page 69 for more in-depth instructions.

Card 1: Writing goal: what is it that you want out of your writing? Fame? Fortune? Validation? Something else?

Card 2: Conflict/fear: what is stopping you from achieving your writing goal?

Essential World Building Questions Spread

```
┌─────┐        ┌─────┐
│     │        │     │
│  1  │        │  2  │
│     │        │     │
└─────┘        └─────┘
```

difference
from our world

relation to
plot

From *Tarot for Fiction Writers* - www.thewritersaurus.com

Spread Fifteen: The Essential World-Building Questions Spread

This spread is good for genres of speculative fiction, such as fantasy, science fiction, and dystopian fiction.

Directions: Shuffle and cut the deck, then lay out two cards in the above formation. Repeat as necessary. Go to page 71 for more in-depth instructions.

Card 1: what is an essential difference between the story world and our regular world?

Card 2: does this difference relate to the plot? How?

One-Card
Wonder Spread

```
┌─────┐
│     │
│  1  │
│     │
└─────┘
```

From *Tarot for Fiction Writers - www.thewritersaurus.com*

Spread Sixteen: The One-Card Wonder Spread (for writer's block)

Directions: if you encounter a blockage while trying to write, move away from your computer and take out your tarot deck (if you're frustrated or stressed, you may want to give yourself a few minutes to relax). Shuffle and cut the deck, then pull out a card. Go to page 73 for more in-depth instructions.

Card 1: This card will give you guidance why you're blocked, and/or how to fix it.

The Card Meanings

One thing that beguiles new tarot users is that everyone seems to have their own interpretations for each card.

There is a good reason for this. Every reader of the tarot applies their own experiences and unique world views to the cards. This is a good thing! Remember, it is YOUR creative unconscious we're trying to unlock, not that of the person who wrote the pamphlet that came with your deck. In fact, you should be writing down your own interpretations of each card, as instructed in exercise 4 on page 15.

That said, it is unrealistic to expect you to generate a unique meaning out of thin air for every card. You need a starting point. I've distilled the card meanings down to their most story-friendly states below. There is a general description for each card, keywords, and its reversed meaning.

The Major Arcana

Below are suggested interpretations for each card of the Major Arcana. Remember, the Major Arcana deals with life-altering, grand-scale events and archetypal images and characters.

There are twenty-two cards in Major Arcana, numbered 0-21.

For each card, I have listed the following information:

Description: This is the description of the common symbols and images usually portrayed on the tarot cards. These symbols and pictures are the keys to remembering the cards' meanings, as well as interpreting them.

Meaning: A general interpretation of the card if it is upright.

Reversed Meaning: A general interpretation of the card when it appears upside down, usually the opposite or an extreme of the upright meaning.

Keywords: These are short phrases and words that sum up the meaning of the card.

A note on the images used in this book:

As noted in the section on choosing a tarot deck, there are countless decks of standard cards out there, each with its own spin on the images. There is no way to accurately describe them all, so I have chosen to not even try. You should have your own deck out and be referring to those images.

I wanted this section to be illustrated, but finding suitable images was a challenge. The easiest thing to do would be to use the Rider-Waite images, which you may remember is the most popular deck. These images have been in the public domain in the United States since at least 2013—but this is being disputed by the company that sells the Rider-Waite deck.

Rather than get in the middle of that, I chose to use other images. Some date as far back as the 1700s. The one drawback is that some of the imagery that is now ubiquitous in the tarot was not in use at the time the pictured cards were illustrated.

0. The Fool

Meaning: A new beginning. The inexperienced hero at the start of the story. He still thinks everything will be easy, poor guy. Still, he has all the potential in the world.

Reversed Meaning: Stupidity, acting out of ignorance, thinking one knows better than others who are more experienced, failure to heed warnings. This action will start off an irreversible series of events that the character will labor to reverse for the rest of the story.

Keywords: Naiveté, ignorance, a clean slate, potential

le Bateleur

1. The Magician

Meaning: Science and alchemy. Using knowledge to affect the world. As Arthur C. Clarke said, "Any sufficiently advanced technology is indistinguishable from magic." Alternatively, the card may represent a con artist or a charlatan.

Reversed Meaning: Bastardization of nature, perversion. Messing with the natural order of things (think *Frankenstein).*

Keywords: Science, alchemy, powerful knowledge, technology, possibility, potential

2. The High Priestess

Meaning: Hidden secrets, prophecy. A revelation that will change a course of action. Feminine insight.

Reversed Meaning: Knowledge that seems important on the surface, but really isn't (red herrings, anyone?), pretension, conceit.

Keywords: Prophecy, revelation

l'Impératrice

3. The Empress

Meaning: Childbirth, the conception of an idea or plan, traditionally feminine virtues, a woman who is nurturing, caring, and warm.

Reversed Meaning: Emotional manipulation, overprotectiveness, problems during childbirth, the abortion of a plan.

Keywords: Feminine virtues, feminine weaknesses

4. The Emperor

Meaning: Traditionally masculine virtues. A strong, tough, unemotional man. Power, authority, stability.

Reversed Meaning: Tyrannical, power-hungry, ruling with an iron fist.

Keywords: masculine virtues, masculine weaknesses

5. The Pope/Hierophant

Meaning: A spiritual leader, perhaps one who advises the character, more accessible than the High Priestess. Good advice.

Reversed Meaning: Manipulation, bad advice given with the intention to gain power or sabotage. Greed for power.

Keywords: Advisor

6. The Lovers

Meaning: Harmony, two parties working together. A romantic partnership begins. Opposites coming together to form a whole.

Reversed Meaning: A bad match, romantic or otherwise.

Keywords: Harmony

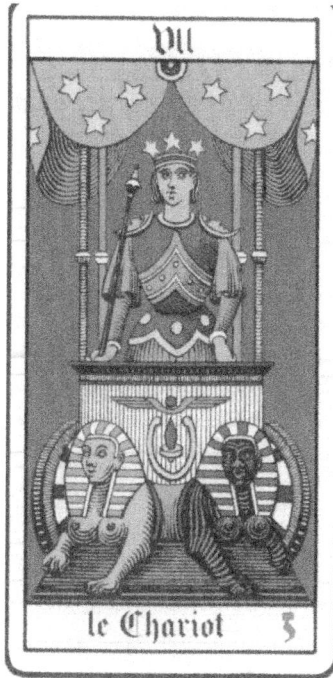

7. The Chariot

Meaning: A necessary war or battle is about to begin, or perhaps a hero is returning from a victory. In either case, the hero is well-prepared.
Reversed Meaning: Defeat, unnecessary war.
Keywords: War, battle, victory

8. Strength

Meaning: Calm in the face of adversity. The character must resolve to do what is necessary, even if it seems impossible or suicidal.

Reversed Meaning: Weakness, fear.

Keywords: Courage

9. The Hermit

Meaning: Separation, old age, voluntary exile. The hermit card may refer to a person, or it may refer to a necessary spiritual or mental journey a character has to undergo. The character may also need to look within rather than without for an answer. This card may relate to the mentor helper in the hero's journey.

Reversed Meaning: Unnecessary separation, disguise, forced exile.

Keywords: Separation

10. The Wheel of Fortune

Meaning: The wheel of fortune represents the ever-changing circle of life. Whenever this card comes up in a reading, consider whether it's time for a paradigm shift. Maybe another character should have a turn at being in power?

Reversed Meaning: The same as above, but perhaps from a different angle.

Keywords: The circle of life, inevitable change

11. Justice

Meaning: The law, fairness. It may mean that the character must accept the consequences for something that they've done, or that the villain is finally going to get his comeuppance.

Reversed Meaning: Unfairness, corruption, bias, nepotism.

Keywords: Law, fairness

12. The Hanged Man

Meaning: An experience gives the character a new perspective on the world, perhaps they encounter someone or something with a viewpoint that contradicts their own. Alternatively: martyrdom, sacrifice, trials. Only rarely will this card refer to actual hanging or execution.

Reversed Meaning: Selfishness, inability to see the obvious.

Keywords: Perspective

13. Death

Meaning: Despite its infamous reputation, the death card should rarely be taken literally (unless you aspire to be the George R. R. Martin of your generation). When using the cards for story development, an exception may be if you're deciding whether or not to kill off a particular character. Usually, the death card signals the end of something. Perhaps a paradigm shift is in order, or a relationship or storyline should be ended.

Reversed Meaning: Stagnation, the inability to change.

Keywords: Ending, change

14. Temperance

Meaning: Everything in moderation. A character may abstain from something as a form of penance.

Reversed Meaning: Religion, churches. The character may have to suffer to achieve a goal.

Keywords: Moderation

15. The Devil

Meaning: Another card that might elicit gasps when it is laid out. The devil rarely refers to Lucifer himself, but refers more to bondage. It can mean a new marriage, relationship, or partnership.

Reversed Meaning: Addiction, the inability to let something go and move on.

Keywords: Entrapment, deals, bondage

16. The Tower

Meaning: As the image suggests, The Tower is the worst card in the Major Arcana. It spells disaster and ruin. The characters may fall victim to a sneak attack. Plans are derailed. This is the "dark moment of the soul" referred to in Campbell's *The Hero's Journey*. Unforeseen catastrophe.

Reversed Meaning: All the above to a lesser degree; imprisonment.

Keywords: Ruin, catastrophe, fall

Ph.
FRANÇAIS
ב
HÉBREU
ק
SANSCRIT
¹/ ○
ÉGYPTIEN
△
ARCHÉOMÈTRE
SAINT YVES

17

☿
⊙
♀
MERCURE

L'ÉTOILE
LES FORCES DIVINES NATURELLES
LA NATURE
FÉCONDITÉ

17. The Star

Meaning: Wishes may soon be fulfilled, though probably not in the way the character expects them to be. Nevertheless, the results are favorable.

Reversed Meaning: Deception, secrecy. Actions that cannot be easily explained.

Keywords: Hope

18. The Moon

Meaning: Secrecy, disguise. Not everything is as it seems. A character gains a new perspective. Supernatural forces may be at work.

Reversed Meaning: delusion, deception, not seeing things the way they really are.

Keywords: Secrecy, perception

19. The Sun

Meaning: The happiest card in the deck. Contentment, joy, peace. One thing to keep in mind while writing is that we don't want our characters to stay happy for very long, lest the story become boring. If you draw this card, it may refer to a character's happier past, or the world they are trying to protect or create.

Reversed Meaning: All the above, to a lesser degree.

Keywords: Happiness, carefreeness

20. Judgement

Meaning: The last battle, which the characters have spent the entire story preparing for. Which side will prevail? Alternatively, resurrection. This card is oddly reminiscent of the character's descent into the spirit world during the climax of the hero's journey.

Reversed Meaning: Punishment for a crime.

Keywords: Outcome

21. The World

Meaning: Assurance of success, travel. The completion of the story.
Reversed Meaning: Stagnation, inability to change.
Keywords: Success, completion

The Cards of the Minor Arcana

As stated earlier in the book, the Minor Arcana deals with everyday personality types and situations.

Each suit corresponds to one of the four elements (fire, water, air, earth), as well as one of the suits of a regular deck of playing cards (clubs, hearts, spades, diamonds). They each contain fourteen cards; four "court" cards and ten numbered cards. Each court card represents a physical description and personality type, and the numbered cards represent an everyday situation. Here is a quick overview of each suit:

The Character Cards, AKA the Court Cards

Below you will find descriptions for each of the sixteen character/court cards. Not all of the information below needs to be taken literally. Drawing a page card *could* refer to a young person, or maybe it refers to an older person who's in a younger frame of mind.

The Court of Wands: The Doers

ROY·DE·BÂTON

King of Wands

Positive character traits (upright): This card is often associated with honesty. A friendly man who has let his passion and desire choose his path in life.

Negative character traits (reversed): A man who shirked his passion for responsibility and is therefore unfulfilled artistically. Because of this he may be in an unhappy marriage. Alternatively, it may signify a man who has been so focused on his passion that he has not taken time to develop his personal life. Either he is not in a relationship, or he is in an unhappy relationship and is unpartnered. May also refer to a man who has been unable to balance his work with his home life.

Careers: A businessman, artist; whatever the field, it was chosen for passion rather than material gain or duty. Despite this, at this point in his career he has achieved a large order of success, either monetarily or status-wise. In either case he is happy and fulfilled.

Keywords: Honesty, passion, action

REYNE·DE·BATON

Queen of Wands

Positive Character Traits (upright): A freedom-loving woman who is creatively gifted, or gifted in her chosen field. She may have a long-term partner, but her lifestyle and/or career takes a priority over that relationship.

Negative Character Traits (reversed): A woman who denied herself the life that she wanted, either through pressure or fear. She may be in an unhappy marriage or relationship, possibly with a dominant partner who does not value her passions. Or she may have shirked the career she wanted for a more financially stable or socially acceptable path, possibly due to pressure from her family. She may exhibit jealousy to others who have chosen to go after their dreams, especially other women. Alternatively, the reversal may refer to a woman who was so focused on her career that she neglected her personal life, as in just about every Hallmark movie ever made.

Careers: A self-made businesswoman, artist, or other career based on your character's individual passion.

Keywords: Independent, creative, passionate

CAVALIER DI BASTON

Knight of Wands

Positive Character Traits (upright): This character is in the prime of their life. The Knight of Wands signifies change; maybe a move or career change, possibly between a job that was unfulfilling to one that is, or vice versa. The Knight of Wands may represent the King or Queen of Wands in an earlier stage of development, an upstart, intern, or young artist on their way up.

Negative Character Traits (reversed): A forced, unwanted change. Perhaps a change to a less fulfilling job for financial reasons. Perhaps the character is at a crossroads where they must choose between what they desire and something that seems safer.

Careers: The knight may be making a job change, or has just started a new job.

Keywords: Transition, change, emigration

Page of Wands

Positive Character Traits (upright): The Page of Wands represents a nascent form of the passion, interest, and artistry seen in the other court of Wands cards. The page is a young boy or girl passionate about a certain subject, art, or career. They may exhibit a certain amount of prodigy or talent for that subject. They are young enough that they have not heard the discouragement and cynicism from family and friends, and therefore express their passion freely.

Negative Character Traits (Reversed): A child whose passions are stifled by a parent who wants them to do something more financially sound, or go into the family business. Alternatively, the child may be a prodigy who has been exploited by their parents, as in child actors or athletes. They may have a secret passion for something else.

Careers: The Page of Wands probably shows an emerging aptitude and affinity for a particular field, skill, or art.

Keywords: Emerging talent, prodigy

The Court of Cups: The Feelers

King of Cups

Positive Character Traits (upright): A mature man who has lived a comfortable, affluent life. His wealth was probably inherited or earned more easily than normal—he has little experience with the harshness of the world. He has a warm, sensuous personality and is quick to share his comforts with others. He probably gives to charity. Though he is not an artist himself, he enjoys the arts.

Negative Character Traits (reversed): A miserly, cold man. He is emotionally stunted and has a hard time connecting with others. Though he has money he lives an austere life, such as Ebenezer Scrooge from *A Christmas Carol*. He may also be sensitive and easily hurt. Alternatively, an expressive man who spends excessively on worldly pleasures.

Careers: A King of Cups character may live off inheritance or be involved with a family business. He may also do charity work or counseling, or may work in a position with a lot of human contact.

Keywords: Comfort, warmth, affluence

REINE·DECOVPES·

Queen of Cups

Positive Character Traits (upright): A warm, sociable woman who lives in relative luxury. She may have been born into a wealthy family, or was able to marry into one because of her looks or attractive personality. Even if she grew up poor, she had a relatively strife-free life. She may be creative or artistic, but probably lacks the entrepreneurial spark of the Queen of Wands, and engages in art for personal fulfillment only. If she works outside the home, it is probably because she wants to, rather than due to financial need. The Queen of Cups may also represent a woman who is emotionally stable and easily able to relate to others. She relates to others easily and therefore has a wide social network around her.

Negative Character Traits (reversed): A vain woman, possibly deceitful and manipulative, especially to keep up appearances. This is a front to hide her own insecurities. She is emotionally needy and always seeks attention and validation.

Careers: The Queen of Cups may refer to a "kept woman," housewife, or stay-at-home mom. She may work in charity or be involved with women's groups or societies (depending on the time-period). A counselor or social worker is another apt job choice.

Keywords: Emotion, caring, beauty

Knight of Cups

Positive Character Traits (upright): A friendly, amiable young man or woman. Probably poetic, graceful, and well-spoken. A dreamer. This young person always has their head in the clouds, but in a general sense, rather than the hyper goal-focused way of the Wands. They have lived an affluent, blessed life, and have many doors open to them. They relate to others easily and therefore have many relationships, both platonic and romantic.

Negative Character Traits (reversed): Crippling indecision. Because they have so many paths available to them, they have a hard time committing to one. They put their energy into several different places rather than just one, and therefore fail to succeed in any of them. They may fall into the trap of comparing themselves to others who have achieved success. They may have a hard time committing themselves to long-term relationships.

Careers: The Knight of Cups may live off of an inheritance or a lover. They have started many projects, but have not found much success in any of them. Alternatively, they may work in a position that uses their ability to relate to others, such as public speaking or sales.

Keywords: Indecision

Page of Cups

Positive Character Traits (upright): An artistic, loving, and insightful boy or girl. They connect easily with others and don't mind being the center of attention. Probably more innocent-seeming than pages from other suits. They tend to be in touch with both the feminine and masculine sides of themselves, whether they are a boy or girl.

Negative Character Traits (reversed): A spoiled boy or girl who manipulates others emotionally. They may have an inflated sense of self-importance, at odds with their feelings of insecurity. They may also be emotionally vulnerable and need a lot of affection.

Careers: The Page of Cups is probably involved in a wide range of activities, but does not excel in them much. They shine when interacting with others, and much of their personal time is taken up by hanging out with friends.

Keywords: Outgoing, emotionally warm

The Court of Swords: The Knowers

King of Swords

Positive Character Traits (upright): A studious, learned man. He is probably in a place of authority, though he may not necessarily be well-off financially. He places more stock in logic and fact than instinct and intuition. He may be perceived as cold and clinical, and not in touch with his emotions. He believes in objective "fact" over subjective "truth."

Negative Character Traits (reversed): He may be so devoted to fact that he follows rules and laws to the letter rather than to their intended purposes, even to the point of amorality. He may have trouble forming meaningful relationships and relating to others on anything but a tertiary level, he probably does not understand why others act "irrationally." Others might call him callous. He may enjoy playing mind games.

Careers: The King of Swords is well suited to being a doctor, lawyer, professor, or any profession that requires study or learning.

Keywords: Intellect, fact, logic

REYNE ·D'ÉPÉE
Queen of Swords

Positive Character Traits (upright): The Queen of Swords is independent and good in a crisis. Unlike the King of Swords, she has a good grasp of both logic and intuition, and while she may be more logical than intuitive, she can use both to her advantage, and better predict the behavior of others. Also unlike the King of Swords, she is good at reading the undercurrents of a room. She is a formidable person and should not be underestimated.

Negative Character Traits (reversed): Jealous and jaded, she is quick to judge others' motivations and actions in the harshest possible terms.

Careers: Much like the King of Swords, the Queen of Swords will likely be a doctor, lawyer, professor, or similar.

Keywords: Intellect, judgement

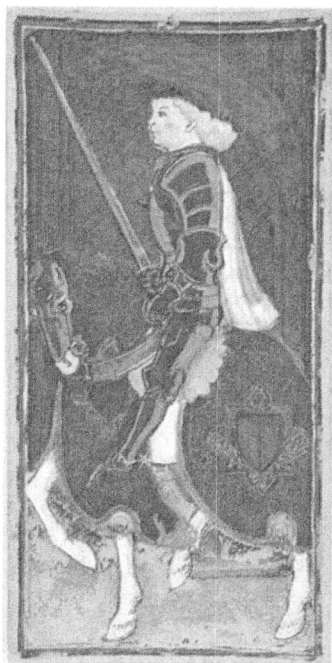

Knight of Swords

Positive Character Traits (upright): An eloquent young man or woman in the prime of life. They are intelligent and can easily become bored. They love a good mystery or puzzle, but may easily become bored and move on if it is not challenging enough.

Negative Character Traits (reversed): They may be prone to arguing, and can often be contrarian even if the other person has good points. They value being right above all else, and some may find them insufferable.

Careers: Seeing as many of the learned professions require years of study, the Knight of Swords will probably still be in school. They may be a graduate student or working towards a PhD.

Keywords: Intellect, learning

Page of Swords

Positive Character Traits (upright): A smart and intelligent child or young person. They are more "book smart" than "street smart," and easily get high marks on tests and papers. They may struggle with the idea that there can be more than one right answer to a problem.

Negative Character Traits (reversed): They may be underachievers, shirking school and homework to study their own personal interests and subjects that prove more of a challenge. Even if they do well in school, they may have trouble making friends and may even be bullied.

Careers: As a student, they are probably in knowledge-based clubs, such as debate, math club, science club, etc.

Keywords: Intellect, knowledge

The Court of Pentacles: The Practical

CAVALIER·DE·DENIERS

King of Pentacles

Positive Character Traits (upright): The King of Pentacles is well-off, but unlike the King of Cups, he is a self-made man. He started from humble means, building his wealth from hard work and a shrewd business sense. He is intelligent, but in a more practical way than the King of Swords. He is most likely a business owner, possibly a family business. He is the patriarch of the family. Despite his wealth, he lives humbly, if comfortably.

Negative Character Traits (reversed): The King of Pentacles is slow to change and mistrustful of innovation. He believes that if something has worked in the past, there is no reason to change his methods. This leaves him vulnerable to sudden shifts and changing technology. It is a weakness his competitors and enemies will take advantage of. Alternatively, the Reversed King of Pentacles may represent a well-off but miserly man, or a man who is unwilling to support his loved ones' choices if they do not coincide with his own beliefs and wishes.

Careers: The King of Pentacles is probably a small business owner, or possibly works in a labor-intensive job related to the earth, such as farming.

Keywords: Shrewdness, practicality, stable, patriarch

REGINA DI DANARI

Queen of Pentacles

Positive Character Traits (upright): The Queen of Pentacles is a practical woman with a good head for business. She is warm and caring, and may splurge on herself every now and then. She is very charitable.

Negative Character Traits (reversed): The reversed Queen of Pentacles is a woman who is suspicious of change and innovation. She may be possessive and jealous of the people around her, especially her children. She may feel the need to "keep up appearances" for the community.

Careers: The Queen of Pentacles may be a homemaker or a small business owner. Whatever it is, she is in charge of her domain.

Keywords: Warm, practical, charitable

Knight of Pentacles

Positive Character Traits (upright): A practical, hardworking man or woman. They would rather work for something than gamble for it. They have a good work ethic and are willing to pay their dues. They have no aversion to tedious tasks, physical work, or hard labor.

Negative Character Traits (reversed): In extreme cases, the Knight of Pentacles may be complacent and lacking in ambition. They may even be boring. Someone who is willing to "climb the ladder" even if there are faster, easier, and better ways to get to the top.

Careers: The Knight of Pentacles may be at community college, learning a trade, or apprenticing under a craftsman. Some may be beginning their own business. If they are going into the family business, they may work closely with a parent.

Keywords: Hard-working, stable

Page of Pentacles

Positive Character Traits (upright): The Page of Pentacles is diligent, patient, and hardworking. Even if they lack talent in a specific area, they are willing to work to get the results they want. They are conscientious.

Negative Character Traits (reversed): The Page of Pentacles could benefit for "working smarter" rather than "working harder." They may need to consider if the work they are doing will yield the results that they desire. In extreme cases, they may not have an end goal in mind at all.

Careers: If they live in the modern era, the Page of Pentacles may have an after-school or summer job; characters in earlier time periods may be laborers, servants, or apprenticing to learn a skilled craft.

Keywords: Patience, diligence

The Situation Cards, AKA the Number Cards

While the Major Arcana depict archetypal characters and moments and the court cards depict personality types, the numbered cards of the Minor Arcana depict everyday situations. The descriptions below follow the same format as the descriptions for the court cards.

Wands

Ten of Wands
Meaning: A burden is bestowed upon someone. Possibly, the burden is initially perceived as a good thing, but is accompanied by hidden consequences.
Reversed Meaning: A hidden person may be working against your character(s).
Keywords: Burden

Nine of Wands
Meaning: This card represents strength in the face of opposition, perhaps because one knows it is necessary.
Reversed Meaning: Unexpected obstacles may occur.
Keywords: Unpleasant surprise

Eight of Wands
Meaning: Taking quick action on a path.
Reversed Meaning: Delays in a course of action.
Keywords: Haste

Seven of Wands
Meaning: Advantage over one's enemies, heated business discussions. The character must be sure to recognize their advantage and use it, lest they lose their ground.
Reversed Meaning: A warning against indecision.
Keywords: Holding your ground

Six of Wands
Meaning: Triumph over an enemy; the deliverance of good news.
Reversed Meaning: Fear, the news of a victorious enemy, an enemy at the gate.
Keywords: Triumph, victory

Five of Wands
Meaning: Imitation, possibly of warfare. Perhaps a con or a farce. Training.
Reversed Meaning: trickery.
Keywords: Imitation

Four of Wands
Meaning: Domesticity, home-making. Perhaps a return to the family estate or a trip to visit relatives. A safe haven.
Reversed Meaning: A domestic peace that is in great danger.
Keywords: Safe haven

Three of Wands
Meaning: Considerable power or wealth that was gained through hard work.
Reversed Meaning: The beginning of a new partnership, perhaps after years of adversity.
Keywords: Prosperity, enterprise

Two of Wands
Meaning: The character is at a crossroads. The decision he makes now will either lead to wealth, riches, and success, or failure, embarrassment, and suffering.
Reversed Meaning: An apparent success that leaves the character unsatisfied or does not have the intended outcome.
Keywords: Choice

Ace of Wands
Meaning: The Ace of Wands represents action, passion, creativity, enterprise.
Reversed Meaning: All the qualities listed above, but in their most perverted and negative forms or taken to extremes: obsession, burnout, neglecting friends and family.
Keywords: Action, passion, creativity, enterprise

Cups

Ten of Cups
Meaning: Utopia. May represent the character's happy home, which was lost long ago or is threatened. Alternatively, it may represent what they hope to gain by achieving their goal. In either case, it is the character's motivation.
Reversed Meaning: Domestic violence, a home or life built under false pretentions.
Keywords: Utopia, happiness

Nine of Cups
Meaning: Satisfaction, eating or consuming to one's heart's content.
Reversed Meaning: Gluttony, wastefulness.
Keywords: Surplus, opulence, satisfaction

Eight of Cups
Meaning: Abandoning a course of action, possibly giving up or switching tactics. May refer to a character letting go of a habit, belief, or goal, possibly one that hindered his success.
Reversed Meaning: Running away from one's troubles rather than staying and fighting. Abandoning responsibilities to chase an impossible dream.
Keywords: Letting go, abandonment

Seven of Cups
Meaning: Turning to supernatural means to solve a problem, prophecy, divine intervention. Alternatively: beliefs that aren't true; delusions.
Reversed Meaning: Desire, will, determination to achieve a dream.
Keywords: Vision

Six of Cups
Meaning: Nostalgia, happiness derived from the past, perhaps childhood.
Reversed Meaning: A future about to come to fruition.
Keywords: Nostalgia, happy memory

Five of Cups
Meaning: Loss, bereavement. The card can also represent a character ignoring what they have left in order to dwell on what they have lost. They may even seek revenge.
Reversed Meaning: Plans that came to fruition, but with only a fraction of the desired results.
Keywords: Loss, glass-half-empty mentality

Four of Cups
Meaning: Dissatisfaction with what one has, desire for more. The character's needs have been met, but not their desires.
Reversed Meaning: Sullenness.
Keywords: Dissatisfaction

Three of Cups
Meaning: Pledges, success, victory. Celebration.
Reversed Meaning: Excess, an end to something.

Keywords: Pledge

Two of Cups
Meaning: A new friendship, partnership, relationship, or marriage. Happy relations between lovers. A new beginning.
Reversed Meaning: Entrapment, a bad match.
Keywords: New relationships

Ace of Cups
Meaning: All that the Cups embody: emotion, human connection, relationships.
Reversed Meaning: Destructive emotion and relationships, unhealthy attachment, sloth, material excess.
Keywords: Emotion, relationships

Swords

Ten of Swords
Meaning: The Ten of Swords indicates pain, fear, suffering, death, perhaps before an escape or change was to be made, ruining a plan.
Reversed Meaning: Short-lived success; counting your chickens before they're hatched.
Keywords: Death, pain, suffering

Nine of Swords
Meaning: Desolation, failure. A character is haunted by memories of the past, or afflicted with mental troubles, such as post-traumatic stress disorder. Inability to move on.
Reversed Meaning: Negative visions, worry for the future.
Keywords: Nightmares, bad memories

Eight of Swords
Meaning: Self-sacrifice as a last resort.
Reversed Meaning: A debilitating affliction that prevents a character from acting as planned.
Keywords: Self-sacrifice

Seven of Swords
Meaning: A last-ditch effort, a plan that may fail. Someone who is a thief or con-man by trade. A heist.
Reversed Meaning: Bad planning.
Keywords: Desperation

Six of Swords
Meaning: A long, arduous journey, perhaps by water. There is no quick way out of this situation, the character must settle in for the long haul.
Reversed Meaning: Fleeing, perhaps in disguise.
Keywords: Journey

Five of Swords
Meaning: Degradation, a victory by unfair means. Playing dirty.
Reversed Meaning: More of the same.
Keywords: Degradation

Four of Swords
Meaning: A knight or warrior (or the equivalent) goes into exile, perhaps voluntarily. It may perhaps hint at peace at the end of a soldier's life, a "good death" in battle.
Reversed Meaning: Sacrificing oneself for a cause.
Keywords: Self-sacrifice, exile

Three of Swords
Meaning: Losing a lover, close friend, or family member. Heartbreak, especially long-term. Loss.
Reversed Meaning: Separation from what you love, perhaps mentally.
Keywords: Heartache, heartbreak

Two of Swords
Meaning: Balance, justice. A deciding force may make a decision that is objectively fair that the character disagrees with. Alternatively, a character may decide to go through some sort of difficult trial for the sake of their friends.
Reversed Meaning: Imbalance, being caught between two opposing forces or viewpoints.
Keywords: Balance, blind justice

Ace of Swords
Meaning: Triumph, perhaps by a force of will. Excess, the spoils of war.
Reversed Meaning: A apparent triumph with disastrous results. The character gets what they want but with unintended consequences.
Keywords: Victory, triumph, intellect

Pentacles

Ten of Pentacles
Meaning: Good family relations. Inheritance. Wealth amassed by generations of work.
Reversed Meaning: Games of chance, gambling with what one has.
Keywords: Inheritance

Nine of Pentacles
Meaning: Safe choices, limited success.
Reversed Meaning: Bad choices, risk.
Keywords: Prudence

Eight of Pentacles
Meaning: Craftsmanship, skill, good business sense.
Reversed Meaning: Lack of ambition, or ambition to manipulate and shirk one's responsibilities, to succeed through dishonest means rather than put in the necessary work.
Keywords: Craftsmanship

Seven of Pentacles
Meaning: Dissatisfaction with one's situation or life. The character may want something more, or think their life's work is not important.
Reversed Meaning: Anxieties about funds.
Keywords: Dissatisfaction

Six of Pentacles
Meaning: Presents, gifts, mercy. The help of someone in a higher position is needed, or perhaps the characters need to think about helping someone else. Receiving one's just reward.
Reversed Meaning: Sabotage masquerading as friendly advice or charity.
Keywords: Gifts

Five of Pentacles
Meaning: Material trouble, obstacles thrown in the way of your characters. Setbacks, generally. Societal Indifference.
Reversed Meaning: The need to seek help.
Keywords: Material trouble.

Four of Pentacles
Meaning: Holding onto one's material wealth. Making safe decisions.

Reversed Meaning: Inability to let go of something, such as possessions, a course of action, or an ideal. Miserliness.
Keywords: Surety, inability to let go.

Three of Pentacles
Meaning: Skilled labor, craftsmanship. Talent and work so superb that it brings a character out of obscurity and into fame, nobility, or royal favor. The character's hard work has paid off, in a sense.
Reversed Meaning: Mediocre work, averageness. Alternatively, someone else will get the credit and reap the benefits of the character's work.
Keywords: Talent

Two of Pentacles
Meaning: Celebration and merriment in the midst of heated trouble.
Reversed Meaning: A character may be faking enjoyment or happiness in order to appease another, possibly the antagonist.
Keywords: Celebration

Ace of Pentacles
Meaning: Wealth, comfort, prosperity, practicality.
Reversed Meaning: The evil side of wealth: greed, miserliness, avarice, inability to change, indifference to the suffering of others.
Keywords: Material wealth, stability, practicality

Using Playing Cards for Tarot Readings

As stated in the section about choosing a tarot deck, you *can* use a regular fifty-two-card deck of playing cards for tarot readings. Many professional card readers do so. Some say it prevents the imagery on the cards from affecting the reading.

The four suits of the Minor Arcana correspond almost perfectly with the four suits of the fifty-two-card deck, except that the fifty-two-card deck lacks the Page cards. They also lack the Major Arcana completely. Finally, they are not illustrated, which makes remembering the cards' meanings harder.

Despite these relative shortcomings, there are instances where you may want to use a fifty-two-card deck for your readings. Perhaps you're traveling and have only playing cards with you, or perhaps you're on the fence about the tarot and want to try a few readings before you commit to purchasing a deck. Maybe you just don't want the card's illustrations to influence your intuition.

One option is to simply read without worrying about the missing cards. However, since the archetypal nature of the Major Arcana may be helpful in your readings, I have created the below list of cards from the fifty-two-card deck that correspond to each card of the Major Arcana. Note that each of these also corresponds to a card from the Minor Arcana. So the King of Spades can mean either the King of Swords or The Emperor.

The Fool (0)—Joker
The Magician (1)—King of Clubs (King of Wands)
The High Priestess (2)—Queen of Spades (Queen of Swords)
The Empress (3)—Queen of Diamonds (Queen of Pentacles)
The Emperor (4)—King of Spades (King of Swords)
The Hierophant (5)—King of Hearts (King of Cups)
The Lovers (6)—Two of Hearts (Two of Cups)
The Chariot (7)—Six of Clubs (Six of Wands)
Strength (8)—Ace of Clubs (Ace of Wands)
The Hermit (9)—Seven of Diamonds (Seven of Pentacles)
Wheel of Fortune (10)—Ace of Diamonds (Ace of Pentacles)
Justice (11)—Six of Diamonds (Six of Pentacles)
The Hanged Man (12)—Any Reversed Jack (Knight)
Death (13)—Four of Spades (Four of Swords)
Temperance (14)—Two of Diamonds (Two of Pentacles)
The Devil (15)—Eight of Spades (Eight of Swords)
The Tower (16)—Ten of Spades (Ten of Swords)
The Star (17)—Ace of Hearts (Ace of Cups)
The Moon (18)—Eight of Hearts (Eight of Cups)
The Sun (19)—Ten of Hearts (Ten of Cups)
Judgement (20)—Two of Spades (Two of Swords)

The World (21)—Queen of Clubs (Queen of Wands)
Page of Wands—Five of Clubs (Five of Wands)
Page of Cups—Four of Hearts (Four of Cups)
Page of Swords—Black Joker
Page of Pentacles—Red Joker

Resources

Books
Waite, A. (American edition, 1998; originally published in the UK in 1910). *The Pictorial Key to the Tarot*. Stanford, Connecticut: U.S. Games.

Dee, J. (1996). *Tarot*. London, England: Barnes and Noble Books.

Lynch, A. (2017). *Mapping the Hero's Journey with Tarot: 33 Days to Finish Your Book*.

Internet Resources
Free printable Court Tarot deck: http://www.darktarot.com/printable_tarot_deck/court_games_tarot.php

Tarot for Fiction Writers Pinterest Board: https://www.pinterest.com/thewritersaurus/tarot-for-fiction-writers/

All tarot-related articles on The Writersaurus (free content constantly being added): ADD LINK

All the public domain images of the 1910 Rider-Waite tarot deck: https://en.wikipedia.org/wiki/Rider-Waite_tarot_deck

Information on the Rider-Waite deck and U.S. Games' copyright claim: http://wildhunt.org/2012/12/the-rider-waite-tarot-deck-and-the-public-domain.html

Another helpful guide to using the tarot for writers: https://writetodone.com/the-tarot-as-a-tool-for-writing-your-novel/

Information on Logos, ethos, and pathos: http://www.pathosethoslogos.com/

Collected tarot Spreads for Writers: http://www.aeclectic.net/tarot/spreads/writers_artists.shtml

Youtube video that shows the weakening of Ron's character in the Harry Potter movies:
https://www.youtube.com/watch?v=IETG9vuHf58&t=104s

Youtube video about Movie Ron vs. Book Ron:
https://www.youtube.com/watch?v=wVBr_TIy9N8

Downloads

To access all the downloads mentioned in this book, please visit
www.thewritersaurus.com/tarot

The Writersaurus Guides Series

Tarot for Fiction Writers
The Fiction Writer's Tarot Journal

For an up-to-date list of books in The Writersaurus Guides series, visit www.thewritersaurus.com/guides.

Also By H. Duke

Jeremiah Jones Cowboy Sorcerer
Season 1, Episodes 1-8 (individual episodes)
Taming the Wolf
The Complete First Season
A Cowboy Sorcerer Christmas

Pagewalker Series
Pagewalker (book 1); Forthcoming
Wordeater (Pagewalker book 2)
Spinebreaker (Pagewalker book 3)

Horror
Things on the Shelf: Three Tales of Christmas Terror

About the Author

Haley Dziuk is the creator and admin of thewritersaurus.com. She has written over ten fiction books under the pen name H. Duke, including the *Jeremiah Jones Cowboy Sorcerer* serial, *Things on the Shelf: Three Tales of Christmas Terror*, and the forthcoming *Pagewalker* series. To see an up-to-date list of her works, visit hdukeauthor.com.

Made in the USA
Coppell, TX
15 February 2022